MW00563861

FROM GUJARAT WITH LOVE

FROM GUJARAT WITH LOVE

100 AUTHENTIC INDIAN VEGETARIAN RECIPES

VINA PATEL

Recipe photography by Jonathan Lovekin

PAVILION

This book is dedicated to my father, my supportive husband Haresh and my three beautiful children Elissa, Aamir and Ravina. I love you always.

Photography credits

Jonathan Lovekin: 22, 33, 47, 53, 54, 57, 60, 64, 67, 71, 73, 74, 79, 82, 87, 89, 90, 97, 103, 105, 107, 111, 113, 115, 116, 119, 121, 124, 129, 133, 135, 136, 141, 145, 147, 148, 154, 156, 161, 171, 173, 182, 189, 192, 195, 197, 203.

Samar Singh Virdi: 2, 6, 10, 12, 16–17, 18, 25, 26, 28, 30, 37, 38–39, 48, 50–51, 62–63, 76, 106, 108–109, 123, 126–127, 151, 158–159, 163, 164–165, 177, 178–179, 186–187, 208.

Page 9: Hari Mahidhar / Shutterstock.com
Page 93: robertharding / Alamy Stock Photo

On the cover:
Recipe photography by Jonathan Lovekin
Textile pattern by Kamlesh V. Makawana
Patan ni Vav, Gujarat by Rahul Gajjar
Breadmaker by Samar Singh Virdi

First published in the United Kingdom in 2021
by Pavilion Books
43 Great Ormond Street
London
WC1N 3HZ

Volume copyright © Pavilion Books Company Ltd, 2021
Text copyright © Vina Patel, 2021

Recipe photography by Jonathan Lovekin and
Samar Singh Virdi

ISBN 9781911663867

A CIP catalogue record for this book is available from the British Library.

10 9 8 7 6 5 4 3 2 1

Reproduction by Rival Colour Ltd., UK
Printed and bound by 1010 International Ltd., China

www.pavilionbooks.com

RECIPE NOTES

- Corn or vegetable oil is used throughout unless specified otherwise.
- When deep-frying the oil is hot enough when a cube of bread turns golden in 30 seconds. Take care not to over-fill your pan.
- Green chillies are always serranos unless specified otherwise.
- Vegetables are medium-sized unless specified otherwise.
- Vegetables are always washed; garlic is always peeled.
- Eggs are medium (US large).
- Mustard seeds are always black unless specified otherwise, although yellow could be substituted.
- Sugar is white unless specified otherwise.
- Salt is according to preference.
- Baking powder and bicarbonate of soda (baking soda) are gluten-free.

CONTENTS

7   Preface

8   Author's Note

13   Gujarat: The Culinary Jewel of India

19   How to Use This Book

20   Cooking Times and Temperatures

21   Essential Ingredients

28   Basic Recipes

38   Chutneys & Other Condiments

50   Salads & Raitas

62   Appetizers

108   Dals & Soups

126   Curries

164   Breads

178   Rice & Khichdi

186   Drinks & Desserts

204   Index

207   Acknowledgements

PREFACE

In September 2017, my elder daughter, Elissa, returned home to keep me company, as she would whenever my husband was out of town – which is much too often. I prepared a meal of her favourite dishes, we enjoyed the meal together, and then she and her younger sister went upstairs to spend some quality sister time together. When I joined them, she said 'Meemez (her nickname for me), dinner was great.' And then exclaimed, 'Why don't you write a cookbook for the family and the world? We would love to preserve all your wonderful recipes and share them as heirlooms with generations to come.'

She gave me a sixty-day deadline to collect all the recipes – many of which were tucked away in a big blue Tupperware box in the pantry – and created an extensive to-do list to keep me focused. When I gave her a look of desperation, she said 'Mom, it's not that hard. You just need to write two recipes per day and you'll be done in two months.' Her deadline was cute and funny but also daunting.

Her motivation and enthusiasm for pushing the issue became something I could no longer ignore. I fell in love with the idea that I could leave a legacy for my kids and all the family members and friends who have enjoyed my cooking over the years. Soon, the excitement of writing a book consumed not only myself but my husband, Haresh, my son, Aamir, and the baby of our family, young Ravina – who still offers plenty of trendy advice that only a teenager can offer! My labour of culinary love over many years has led to this: a collection of recipes that I am so proud to share with you.

I felt very honoured that my children requested I write a cookbook to preserve all my recipes, and I began to realize how every recipe of mine was so special to my family and friends. They are the products of many years of trial and error; they are a collection of thirty years of flavours I had picked up, extracted and learnt from my travels all over the world. I realized how much I wanted to share Gujarati food with the rest of the world. I am so proud of our deep heritage, identity and traditions, all of which have informed the person I am today. It has become my mission to bring Gujarati cuisine to those outside our beautiful land and to invite readers to discover the wealth of our rich, vibrant culture.

Of course, while we played with the idea for a cookbook only a few years ago, my story with food began much, much earlier…

AUTHOR'S NOTE

I grew up in Gujarat, a state in western India, as the youngest of five children with a fourteen-year age gap, making me as young as my own nieces and nephews! I had a wonderful, carefree childhood, indulged by my protective and affectionate parents. My father was a magnificent man who was something of a local hero in my community after building a grain-manufacturing empire throughout Vadodara, Surat and Amritsar in Punjab. He was a risk-taker (much like me), but I value another inherited quality even more: his passion for good quality and produce. As a child, I would play among the grains, rice and beans at his food-processing mill and proudly observe his painstaking attention to detail. He taught me about testing the quality of grains and would insist on purchasing produce from only the finest farmers – advice I still value today.

As we were a large family, plenty of people gathered to prepare the humble feasts and I was blessed to be around the women in our immediate family, who were all fantastic cooks. I would simply sit back, watch the dishes being prepared, and enjoy delicious meals all day, every day. Being the youngest member of the family, this was my only assigned role in the kitchen; everyone else cooked. So, while I had never spent a single day cooking in the kitchen as a child, I silently observed everyone, and listened intently to their conversations about ingredients, ideas, methods and techniques.

Fast forward to 1989 when I was in my twenties, got married, and moved to the USA. Cooking for my husband at our home in Santa Cruz, California, was – in hindsight – sheer hilarity! What a mess! Mortified that I had to ditch my first attempt at cooking a meal, combined with the fact that my darling husband had worked all day and come home to a disaster, and a determination and passion to perfect Gujarati-inspired vegetarian home cooking was born.

In addition to becoming a cook, I had to learn to drive, run a household and acclimatize to the customs of a new country. The turning point was when I became a mother for the first time. Our beautiful daughter Elissa was born within a year of my arrival in the States and this changed everything. Driven mostly by a desire not to feed her anything processed or 'from a jar', I took a few basic cooking courses – and the rest was up to me to make it work. The feeling of panic and being overwhelmed was soon replaced with pure excitement: excitement to feed Elissa only the best. When I steamed peas and spinach, and boiled carrots, everything was timed precisely to ensure no nutrients were lost.

Then our wonderful son Aamir arrived. And, several years later, we were blessed with another cute daughter, Ravina. I was determined to recreate the delicious and nutritious food of my own childhood for my growing family. I painstakingly cooked, recooked, developed and tested each recipe until I had perfected the dishes in this book. Hours were devoted to research and spent on long-distance phone calls to relatives in India. But most importantly, as my own worst critic, I whiled away many days and nights seeking perfection from my own recipes. I am often considered a perfectionist, and admittedly at times to my own detriment.

Whether it's remembering the dishes my mother and grandmother nourished us with, snacks and spreads at weddings and festivals, or restaurants throughout the world that

- મેથીનો મસાલો . ૨૦૦ ગ્રામ ૧૦૦/-
- ચાટ મસાલો . . . ,, ૧૦૦/-
- સંભાર મસાલો . ,, ૧૦૦/-
- મસાલા ચાણા . . ,, ૧૦૦/-
- સાદા ખાખરા . . ૫૦૦ ગ્રામ ૧૮૦ રૂ.
- મસાલા ખાખરા . ,, ૧૮૦/-
- મેથીના ખાખરા . ,, ૧૮૦/-
- લીંબુનું અથાણું . ૫૦૦ ગ્રામ ૧૫૦ રૂ.
- આથેલા મરચા . ૫૦૦ ગ્રામ ૧૫૦ રૂ.
- કેરીનુ અથાણું . . ૫૦૦ ગ્રામ ૧૫૦ રૂ.
- રોઝ સરબત ખસ સરબત ૧ બોટલ ૧૮૦ રૂ.
- આદુ લીંબુ સરબત ,, ૨૦૦ રૂ.
- હંકાઇ . . . . . . ,, ૩૦૦ રૂ.

my husband and I have had the privilege to visit, I never stop thinking about food and cooking. I never stop thinking about Gujarat either. It's not just the sights and sounds of Gujarat that have me craving my homeland, it's the unmistakably unique aromas and flavours of my native cuisine that bring a deep longing – a nostalgia so powerful, it's hard to put into words. Recreating the dishes from my youth, I am catapulted back in time, as if I am standing with my parents and grandparents in their kitchen … watching, listening, smelling, tasting.

I am constantly inspired. My husband and I regularly return to Gujarat, and each trip 'home' is a sensory overload. Much to my kids' annoyance, I can still be found harassing chefs, asking questions about ingredients and techniques, and picking their brains about the dish I am enjoying. Scribbles for recipe ideas on napkins and in notes on my phone collected over the years led to an arsenal of indispensable recipes I use to recreate and perfect authentic Gujarati dishes in my American kitchen, ensuring the freshest ingredients are used and preparing them in such a way to optimize nutritional value.

I have always been deeply inspired by the late Julia Child, who did so much to introduce French cooking to American kitchens. My goal is similar: to share the wonder of the Gujarati cuisine with the world. Quite a feat for someone with a professional background in finance! And while I've encountered my fair share of criticism for having this ambition, I am a tenacious woman on a mission, marching in the face of adversity. If I can inspire just one other woman to follow her dreams, value her goals, and work towards the vision that burns brightly in her heart (regardless of age or background), then I have done my job.

I learnt a very important thing about good food and cooking. It's not so much about making the perfect recipe. It's about the enthusiasm for perfecting it and the enjoyment experienced when sharing it with others. Typical of me as a host, it's deeply satisfying when forty-plus friends are in my kitchen watching me prepare a newly discovered dish, eagerly firing away questions about what I am doing and asking me how they came to be so lucky to deserve this meal. I particularly love the rustic, no-nonsense manner of serving straight from my pan onto their plates, creating a wonderfully casual eating environment. They can see the passion and love that goes into it and I know they can taste it too. Cooking and feasting bring friends and strangers together. Putting a smile on their faces and good food in their bellies is all I have ever wanted – and it's still all I desire. There is no need for fine china: the food will speak for itself. Simply cook from the heart. I am neither doctor nor celebrity, I am just a woman who keeps her beautiful family happy by ensuring they are nourished and always eager to learn.

I have put my heart and soul into this book. It features a cherry-picked collection of one hundred authentic vegetarian dishes, to celebrate and savour, and all carefully chosen and modified to suit the western home cook. Some of these dishes acknowledge friends and family, others honour those no longer with us. But most importantly, this book is a tribute to Gujarat: a place I called home for more than twenty years. While my focus is on Gujarati cuisine, I'm so excited to share some interesting vegetarian recipes from many countries I have travelled. But this book is truly a window into the heart and soul of Gujarati cuisine, and I believe it's fittingly titled *From Gujarat with Love*. I hope you enjoy preparing these vegetarian recipes in your home as much as I have.

GUJARAT: THE CULINARY JEWEL OF INDIA

My homeland of Gujarat is fondly referred to as the jewel of western India. It boasts a population of sixty-four million people but the fifth-largest state is often overlooked by tourists visiting India. Those who have visited have been welcomed by the warm hospitality of Gujaratis (informally known as Gujjus), witnessed the breathtaking landscape, and feasted on the exceptional cuisine.

Gujarat is India's western-most state, facing the Arabian Sea on one side and bordered by Pakistan (north); Rajasthan (northeast); the enclaves of Dadra, Nagar Haveli, Daman and Diu (south); Maharashtra (southeast); and Madhya Pradesh (east). It is the birthplace of many notable Indians, including Mahatma Gandhi, the poet Narsinh Mehta, as well as the father of India's space programme, Vikram Sarabhai. The Indian prime minister, Narendra Modi, and the late business tycoon Dhirubhai Ambani and his son Mukesh (who happens to be the richest man in India), also grew up in Gujarat. We also have some very notable cultural figures. Farrokh Bulsara, who became Freddie Mercury, the inimitable frontman of the rock band Queen, may have been born in Tanzania, but his parents hailed from Valsad (formerly Bulsar) and Freddie was fluent in Gujarati.

As a state Gujarat is diverse and vibrant, where past and present converge to form a region deeply rooted in art, heritage and culture – but its food culture is my pride and joy. Like many cuisines from around the world, the food and diet of Gujarat have been uniquely shaped by geography, climate, history and religious beliefs. Over the centuries, the state has been ruled by Marathas, Rajputs, Mughals, other invading Islams and the Mauryans. Moreover, as a prominent port state, the Gujarati culture had also been influenced by international trade beyond its immediate neighbours. As a result, many styles of cooking and spices have been incorporated into our food traditions.

VEGETARIANISM

While there are some communities within the state that do eat meat, the vast majority of Gujaratis are vegetarian. We have to thank the deep history of vegetarian cooking for informing the modern recipes of today.

Plant-based diets are common in Gujarat because of the influence of Jainism, an ancient Indian religion originating in the sixth century. Jains cannot consume anything that is the result of injuring or killing another living thing, which means no meat or other animal products including gelatine or eggs. Even root vegetables, such as onions and garlic, are forbidden because their removal from the ground is considered an act of killing another living thing. It has been said that Jainism has one of the most influential impacts on vegetarianism across Indian culture.

So, while Gujarati cuisine is informed by Jainism, our vegetarian diet tends to be slightly more relaxed. We take advantage of the abundance of locally grown vegetables in the region, and our modern diets include dairy (notably ghee, cheese and yogurt) and root vegetables. I may be biased, but Gujarat is a food-lover's paradise because our cuisine is unlike any other in India.

REGIONAL CUISINES

Strolling through local streets anywhere in Gujarat can only be described as a welcome assault on all the senses. Sweet, bold aromas, vibrant colours and the tasty food to be enjoyed at every corner is paradise for those who truly appreciate unique cooking styles. Gujarati cuisine is elaborate, the flavours multi-dimensional, if erring on the sweet side.

Ahmedabad

As the largest city in Gujarat, Ahmedabad has a thriving, pulsating street-food culture offering exciting snacks and small plates. When Indians consider Gujarati cuisine, they often reference the flavours of this city. Favourite dishes include White Dhokla, a steamed gram – besan or chickpea – flour snack (page 80), garnished with coriander (cilantro), jalebi (deep-fried spiral-shaped dough dipped in a sweet syrup); and golas (granita/snow cones dipped in rich syrups). Khandvi (page 66), made from chickpea batter, is cooked and thickened to a paste, then rolled out and served with chutney.

Surat

The former seaport of Surat is popularly known for its diamond cutting-and-polishing trade but feasting on the unique and delicious Surti snacks should be top priority for food lovers! Located in south Gujarat, Surat's cuisine spans the realm from street food to fine dining. Surat's signature dish is Undhiyu (page 162). Indian flat beans (papdi), pigeon peas, potatoes, aubergine (eggplant), purple yam, bananas and spices are combined in an earthen pot, then covered and buried in the ground. It is then surrounded by coal and slow-cooked with an infused smoky flavour. Undhiyu is generally prepared in winter when flat beans and purple yams are in season.

Kathiyawad

Kathiyawad forms part of the region known as Saurashtra, which includes major cities such as Porbandar, Bhavnagar, Jamnagar, Rajkot and Junagadh. The food here tends to be more spicy.

Kutch

Kutch is a dry and arid district in northwest Gujarat without leafy vegetation. Here, you'll find street-food dishes such as Dabeli (page 94) – pao or a bread roll stuffed with a potato and tamarind filling. It is then roasted and finished with sev (a popular Indian noodle snack). Bajra na rotla (Pearl Millet Bread, page 176) is a type of Indian flatbread made of pearl millet, and khaja – a sweet layered fritter dipped in syrup – is a local favourite.

THE FLAVOURS OF GUJARAT

Throughout India, whenever anyone takes a bite of food they taste the flavour of Gujarat. That flavour comes from the salt (sabras) – as almost 80 per cent of Indian sea salt is harvested in this one state. There is a tradition here during Diwali: at dawn on New Year's Day, salt-sellers can be heard wandering through residential areas and calling 'Sabras lo!' They are given baksheesh (cash) in return for a handful of salt crystals. The housewife mixes the sabras in her kitchen salt jar and switches on the Diwali lights. The salt brings flavour to her food but also the promise of good luck and year-round prosperity to her family.

Gujaratis are famous for their sweet tooth. (Sugar is a food that is said to help with hydration, which is essential, living in a hot dry climate, and people are accustomed to adding sweetness.) To keep that sweet tooth happy, the Gujju housewife almost always sprinkles a spoonful of sugar or pops a small ball of jaggery into savoury dishes she cooks – dal served in a Gujju home has a typically sweetish-spicy taste. And ice cream has become a must-have among urban Gujaratis – a few decades ago it would have been a culinary impossibility but now it's all the rage with vegetarian foodies. On summer evenings after a meal, many families take a trip to their favourite ice-cream outlet, a custom that's almost as important as making the pilgrimage to Shrinathji's Temple in Nathdwara!

Located on the south-western coast of Gujarat, Bharuch and Khambhat became major trading posts for India. Sweet and sour flavours were popular along the hot and humid coastline. The port scene was a melting pot, where Arabs entered the state and departing Gujaratis made their way to Europe, East Africa, the Middle East and South Asia. While many merchants sought new fortunes, they also shared and collected recipes on their journeys. In fact, Mahatma Gandhi was among those travellers. Born in Porbandar, Gujarat, Gandhi had a major influence on the cuisine. While the state of Gujarat was largely vegetarian, Gandhi's success in the practice of non-violence further popularized the plant-based diet.

meaning they're light and irresistible. Two quintessential farsan are Khandvi (melt-in-the-mouth rolls made with besan and buttermilk, page 66) and Nylon Khaman (yellow sponges, page 77).

The Hindu festival Navaratri is a glorious event lasting nine nights and ten days, celebrated by dancing and feasting. Gujarati thalis (see the box on page 106) offer a chance to showcase more than a dozen little farsans and sweet dishes (mithais). These strictly adhere to dietary rules according to the combinations of food being served. Navaratri falls during the month of Ashvin (at the beginning of October) to mark the harvest, and nightly celebrations include the dance of the sticks, the Dandiya Raas.

For special events and traditional Gujarati weddings alike, food is placed on a long table with guests seated on one side. The hosts stand at the table and humbly serve their guests throughout the celebration until the feast is over. And what a feast. The food is often placed directly in a guest's mouth, despite their overindulged belly!

Appetizers (Farsan)

The appetizers in this book are all traditional, uniquely spiced snacks that together form what is known as farsans. In India this is as much a tradition as eating tapas in Spain, or mezze in Greece, where small plates are put together to form a larger spread at formal and informal events. And Gujarat is far and away the leader: Gujarati farsans are enjoyed the length and breadth of India, including at Punjabi weddings! Many of the plant-based dishes use gluten-free gram (besan or chickpea) flour and some are steamed,

HOW TO USE THIS BOOK

Above everything else, this book is a celebration of Gujarat and my relationship with its food and culture. For those of you who are new to the cuisine, I've provided essential ingredients and basic recipes – such as the ubiquitous Coriander-cumin Powder (page 29) and Pickle Masala (page 34) – to get you started, but all of them can be found in Indian supermarkets. In fact, many Gujaratis prefer to buy these two specific ingredients in shops, but I've provided them here as a Gujarati cookbook would feel incomplete without them.

Gujarat's history is as rich and vibrant as its culture, and it made sense to share the wealth of the region with my readers. One of the greatest challenges when I first started the book was deciding what to include – there are just too many to love! I have highlighted some of our most iconic dishes, such as Shrikhand (page 194), and notes of our fascinating history are peppered throughout the book.

A few additional elements have been included to make the recipes as user-friendly as possible. The prep and cooking times will help you stay organized and on schedule in the kitchen, while dietary information is indicated as below.

- GF   **Gluten-free**

- DF   **Dairy-free**

- VG   **Vegan**

- Q   **Quick and easy** (30 minutes or less)

COOKING TIMES
AND TEMPERATURES

I was somewhat perplexed recently when I sampled dishes that my husband and mother-in-law created following my own recipes. They weighed the ingredients accurately and they did as they were instructed when following my methods, but the outcome of their dishes was simply not what it should have been.

I spotted the error one night when my husband was cooking. 'Turn down the heat,' I yelled – and then the proverbial penny dropped: they were cooking some ingredients at too high a temperature!

Cooking over a low heat (particularly onion and tomato curries) is critical for the retention of flavour, texture and colour. Failing to do so will yield a different, undesired result. Keep the heat low until the rawness of onions and tomatoes disappears. I cannot stress enough how important it is to cook at the right temperatures.

You will notice I use a pressure cooker in a lot of my recipes. I do this purely for time management, but you could get the same results in a pan on the stovetop – you will just need to cook for a longer time to achieve the same results.

Most of my recipes can be cooked in under 30 minutes – which really isn't a long time. However, many people still feel tempted to cook over high heat to get food on the table more quickly. This will do an injustice to the ingredients – especially spices, which need to

be cooked over a low heat so they can settle and absorb into the other ingredients, allowing for a richer, more pleasing end result.

Having this extra time can be seen as a very positive thing! It allows you the time to get on with other chores in the kitchen, which we often overlook. Take the time to clean your kitchen (this makes for a much less stressed, more organized cook) and perhaps get a headstart on stacking the dishwasher. You could set the table for your family (this makes a much better dining experience) and even have a little time to catch up with family members while they are drawn to all the wonderful smells coming from your kitchen.

Curries and dals should also be cooked in medium-sized, deep-based saucepans, not frying pans or skillets. Saucepans allow the moisture to be retained and will accommodate the volume of the dishes being prepared.

In essence, you want to produce a dish that is full of the best flavours your ingredients can deliver and served with the most superb texture that does it justice.

Remember: never rush a good thing. Not only will your food smell and taste better, but it will look more attractive too.

ESSENTIAL INGREDIENTS

In order to truly replicate and enjoy the authentic flavours of any food culture, it's important to familiarize yourself with the spices, the produce and other ingredients that capture its essence. Here are some of the most commonly used in Gujarati cooking that appear throughout the book.

Ajwain/ajmo (carom) seeds: These bring a bittersweet flavour and are often included when cooking gas-inducing foods including dried or fresh pulses, such as gawar, valor and papdi. A spoonful of coarsely ground ajwain seeds taken with water is a traditional home remedy for indigestion or mild stomach upsets.

Asafoetida: Harvested as the dried gum or resin from the roots of the ferula plant (one of the celery family), asafoetida powder plays a small but significant part in Indian cooking. It is a strong digestive and preservative. It is used as the last ingredient to be put in the tadka, immediately before the tempered hot oil is poured over a curry, dal or vegetables. A pinch is all that is required; the fragrant aroma released as it hits the hot oil will permeate the final dish. This aroma is completely different from the smell of asafoetida in its raw form, which not many people enjoy!

Bajra flour: Bajra is a pearl millet widely grown and consumed extensively across parts of rural India as the thick flatbreads known as Rotlo, plural Rotla (page 176). The grain is a rich source of fibre, magnesium and potassium that helps keep the heart healthy, the blood pressure normal and maintains cholesterol levels. No wonder bajra is now hailed as a superfood. As both a grain and a flour, bajra is used in many other ways in Gujarati cuisine: as vada (Spicy Potato Croquettes, page 98), in Pearl Millet Bread (page 176) and as pudla (pancakes) served for breakfast.

Besan (gram or chickpea) flour: Besan is a staple of Gujarati cooking and with good reason: it is high in protein and fibre, contains a multitude of nutrients and helps digestion, making it ideal to eat at the beginning of a meal. It features in many of my recipes.

Betel leaves: Served with areca nut and various condiments, betel leaf, known as paan, can be chewed after a meal as a kind of mouth freshener and digestive. Sometimes tobacco is added and that's when it becomes addictive. Betel leaf itself has several health benefits, helping to lower blood sugar and increase the body's metabolic rate. The herb is also used in Ayurveda (the ancient Indian medical system) and can be applied topically for near-instant relief from inflammation, aches and pain. It can also be used to treat cuts and boils.

Black gram/black chickpeas (kala chana): These are some of the oldest-known lentils used in Indian cuisine. A nutrients and protein powerhouse, kala chana is soaked overnight or for a few hours, boiled in water and then made into a curd-based curry or a dry sabzi (vegetable dish) flavoured with sautéed onions and garlic.

Black onion seeds/nigella seeds: Popular of late for use in salads, smoothies and other curry dishes.

Cardamom, pods and ground: Whole cardamoms are the small pods, black or

green, that contain the aromatic seeds. Opt for the sweeter green cardamom, which is mostly grown in spice gardens in Kerala, south India. It is used to lightly spice savoury dishes or emphasize the richness of traditional Indian desserts, including Kheer (page 199), Shrikhand (page 194), the sweet flatbread Puran Poli (page 169) and Ladoo (page 202) – one of India's most popular sweets.

Chaat powder: What would we do without chaat masala? This sweet-sour citrusy spice mix containing fennel and coriander seed and powdered green mango (amchur) is what attracts everyone to the wondrous world of chaats – the chatpata snacks served on street-food stalls in cities, towns and villages throughout north India.

Charoli nuts: These are the nuts of the chironji tree, which is widely cultivated in northwest India. Although charoli (or chironji) nuts are considered the poor man's almonds they are low in fat and high in protein and Vitamin B complex. They are mainly used in traditional Indian sweets. Charoli nuts become rancid very quickly so only buy small quantities and store them in the fridge.

Chillies: Fresh and dried, chillies are integral to Indian and Gujarati cooking and are available in various shapes, sizes and colours. The smaller, darker and thinner the chillies are, the more spiciness they bring, so add them carefully.

Coconut: This Indian fruit is amazingly versatile. The water from both the green and the ripe coconut is rich in nutrients and minerals. Its freshly grated coconut flesh, along with chopped fresh coriander (cilantro), garnishes many savoury dishes, whereas coconut milk, a processed product, rarely

features in Gujarati cuisine; by and large the readily available packets of desiccated (dried shredded) coconut are used. Koprapaak, made from desiccated coconut, sugar and curd (khoya) flavoured with powdered cardamom is one of the sweet-toothed Gujaratis' favourite treats!

Coriander seeds: Generally roasted and coarsely crushed or powdered before use. In powdered form, coriander pairs well with cumin powder and in Gujarati cooking it is largely used in this combination, which is known as dhana-jeeru (page 29).

Cumin seeds: Cumin seeds generally go into the hot oil of the tadka with mustard seeds but sometimes, and in most north Indian dishes, they are used on their own. Cumin has cooling and digestive properties. During the hot Indian summers roasted cumin seeds are ground to a powder and added to cold buttermilk for a refreshing drink. Sprinkled on chaats with curd (such as dahi-bhalla or dahi-sev-puri), this simple powder transforms a savoury snack from ordinary to extraordinary!

Curry leaves: Fresh curry leaves are integral to south Indian cuisine, but are used in Gujarati dishes too. These small dark green leaves release an interesting bittersweet flavour as they boil in dal or curry or crackle in the hot oil of a tadka for dals, curries or chutneys. Curry leaves bring medicinal benefits as well; their antioxidant and antibacterial properties benefit the digestive tract. Substitute dried if you cannot find fresh curry leaves.

Dates: In Gujarati cuisine, dried dates (kharek) are used largely as a natural sweetener. Kharek is available crushed, chopped or powdered and is often used as prasada (offering) in a religious ceremony or ritual. Fibre-rich and packed with nutrients, dried dates have good digestive properties.

Dried split pigeon peas (tuvar/toor/arhar dal): This is the dal that drives India, sometimes mixed with chana (chickpea/garbanzo), yellow mung (moong), or split red lentil (masoor) dal, especially in north Indian cuisines. The pulse is grown extensively in Gujarat where toor dal is popularly served for lunch in almost all homes – each household will have its own way of cooking it. Toor dal can be bought oiled and unoiled. The oiled version is preferred for its better keeping qualities, an important consideration for Gujarati families who are used to buying their annual supplies of wheat, rice, groundnut (peanut) oil, jaggery and toor dal at harvest time.

Eno (fruit salt): Despite its name, this product contains bicarbonate of soda (baking soda) and citric acid, which is completely safe for use in cooking. All Gujarati kitchens have sachets of Eno fruit salt handy, not to relieve indigestion, acidity, bloating or flatulence, but to make their flours rise and add fluffiness to steamed dishes such as Dhokla (page 80).

Fennel seeds: Largely used in certain masala mixes but rarely alone in Gujarati cooking. Roasted and lightly salted, they have excellent digestive qualities and make a popular after-meal mouth freshener, rather than the sugar-coated mukhwas, which appears in every Gujarati home. Crushed coarsely and soaked in water, then mixed with sugar or honey and served with ice in a tall glass, the seeds make an ideal drink to quench thirst and cool the body naturally in the hot Gujarati summer.

Fenugreek leaves: Bunches of fresh, green fenugreek flood Indian markets in the short winter months. But they disappear once the heat of the long summer makes itself felt. Fresh fenugreek is used to make flavoursome curries, steamed dumplings, and flatbreads including spicy parathas and dhebras (also known as theplas). Again, use dried (kasuri methi) if you cannot find fresh leaves.

Fenugreek seeds: In some households, a pinch of fenugreek seeds is used in the tadka for dals and vegetables. These seeds become crisp when they fry in the hot oil and introduce an interesting bitter crunch to a dal or vegetable dish.

Garlic scapes: The stalks and long leaves of the garlic plant are known as green garlic or scapes and sold in bunches over the short Gujarati winter. The finely cut scapes are added to theplas, vegetables and curries to make the most of this flavourful and health-giving veg during the few weeks when it is available. Packed with nutrients and bad-cholesterol-lowering capabilities, scapes are an excellent addition to vegetarian meals. During the scapes season, one tasty addition to the dinner menu is hot bajra rotla, a flatbread made with garlic scapes sautéed in ghee and served with grated jaggery. It can be found in the frozen section of Indian food markets.

Ghee: No other product can replace ghee – 'clarified butter' is a very distant and poor cousin. Ghee is ghee. Preferably homemade. Let the fresh whole milk (buffalo's or cow's) simmer over a low heat so that the cream rises happily to the top, then allow it to thicken and solidify in the fridge before carefully removing it to another vessel. Repeat the process with the fresh milk you get every day, gathering the cream in the same vessel. If all this is too much work, ghee is available in a tin. Ghee once got a lot of bad press as the reason for high rates of bad cholesterol among Indians. Now ghee is crowned the new 'superfood'!

You need to look for desi ghee, which is made from healthy saturated fats, not hydrogenated refined oil.

Jaggery: Made by boiling sugarcane juice to evaporate the water, jaggery (or gur), the resultant brown solidified mass, has an earthy flavour and is packed with iron and other minerals. It is a natural sweetener used in almost all Gujarati cooking and it is far healthier than using processed sugar. Grated jaggery, rubbed into a spoonful of warm ghee and eaten with bits of roti, is a favourite of Indian toddlers. There are now organic and nutrient-enriched jaggery options available.

Mung beans: These pulses are high in protein, fibre, minerals, iron, calcium and vitamins. They are easily digested so split mung/moong dal (yellow) is always given to senior citizens

and those recovering from illness and is used to wean infants and toddlers. As sprouts, mung beans are very healthy, almost doubling the available nutrient content, especially the antioxidants and amino acids.

Mustard seeds: These take pride of place in the masala dabba, the multi-compartment spice box found in every Indian kitchen. These small black seeds (raido are the bigger ones, rai are the tiny, really fiery, ones) pop and splutter in the little pan used to prepare the tadka (tempering or seasoning) of hot oil before they are poured, crackling and smoky, into a dish. Does half a teaspoon of black mustard seeds heated in oil really enhance the flavour of a panful of dal or vegetables? Absolutely. Next time, make the dish without this crucial seasoning and taste the difference!

Poppy seeds: These minute seeds are a powerhouse of essential minerals – calcium, iron, magnesium, manganese, phosphorous and zinc. They aid sleep and reduce anxiety. In Indian cooking, they are generally used in paste form, made by soaking them in milk then grinding, adding a lovely richness to the curries. Traditional sweets, such as Ladoo (page 202), are often rolled in poppy seeds.

Rice flour/brown rice flour: Rice is a staple across India, especially in coastal regions, eaten daily as a meal of boiled rice with dal or curried vegetables or meats. Gujarat has its own dal-bhaat, a porridge-like mixture of rice and dal, but rice flour is used in many dishes too. Post-harvest, sacks of broken rice are sold at market. This is ground into flour and made into khichi na papad, and stored ready

to be eaten, roasted or fried, throughout the year. The steamed flour, flavoured with ajwain (carom) seeds, ground green chillies and salt, served with a little cold oil poured over, makes a filling snack.

Rose essence: Rose is a natural, traditional cooling ingredient, much appreciated across India for its flavour and medicinal properties. The essence from the local, 'Desi' varieties of edible red and pink roses imparts perfume and taste to foods flavoured with their crushed petals, including milk-based sweets, such as Gulab Jamuns (page 196), soft balls made with wheat flour (maida) and milk solids (khoya) and the little dumplings known as rasgulla, made with whole milk curds and sugar. Another traditional favourite, gulkand is a preserve of crushed fresh rose petals and sugar that is left in the sun to gently cook over weeks.

Split red lentils (masoor dal): On its own, masoor dal is not very popular in Gujarati cuisine; it is generally combined with other dals to add body to a curry. It is sometimes used in lentil-based snacks, including Handvo (page 96), Muthiya (page 91), puda and Dhokla (page 80).

Surti lilva: When the shells of the surti papdi are discarded and only the beans are used, they are known as surti lilva. There are several ways in which these beans are cooked – as a curried vegetable, as a rice biryani, a masala khichdi, and so on. Since these are not available throughout the year, many lilva-lovers freeze them for use after the season is over.

Surti papdi: With the shape of a small curve, this variety of flat bean is available in the winter months only. It is 'topped and tailed' to remove the slightly tough strings, so that the bean can be easily shelled whole, keeping the shells intact. Both the whole shell and the beans are cooked, generally with small aubergines (eggplants) and potatoes. Surti papdi is the most important ingredient in the famous Undhiyu of Surat (page 162).

Tea: This is the drink all of India wakes up to, takes one too many breaks for at work, and is the standard cure for boredom headaches. For an instant pick-me-up, the enduring favourites brewed by the ubiquitous tea stalls known as larris or tapris are milky-sweet concoctions spiked with freshly grated ginger and chai masala powder. The main choice is mamri – a special Assam CTC (crush, tear, curl) black tea that is granular, as opposed to leaf tea – which can withstand extensive boiling to extract flavour. It needs just a cloud of milk,

and is served in a tea service, preferably with honey rather than sugar.

Turmeric, ground: This vivid yellow spice is a health power-tank and a jarful of the powder resides in every Indian kitchen cupboard. Harvested as a root vegetable, boiled, dried and then pulverized into powder, ground turmeric has incredible antiseptic, immunity-boosting and other healing properties because of its basic ingredient, curcumin. Half a teaspoon of turmeric in a glass of warm milk or hot water is guaranteed to soothe a sore throat, control a cold and generally make us feel better.

Tuver lilva (shelled pigeon peas): Green pigeon peas are generally consumed by the truckload in central and south Gujarat during the winter months. Shelling them is a painstaking task but the small jewel-like green gems are worth the effort. Besides the traditional dry vegetable served with small aubergines and the ever-popular lilva ni khichdi, the bite-sized hot-off-the-pan lilva ni kachori with tangy chutney and hot masala chai on winter afternoons is what foodie Gujjus live for!

Valor papdi: A close cousin of surti papdi, the valor papdi (helda bean) is much longer and the shell is much thicker while its beans are flatter. Therefore, the beans are cut into 2.5cm (1-inch) pieces, making them easier to cook. Papdi is always cooked with some ajwain in the tempering oil as the beans can cause gas/flatulence.

BASIC RECIPES

No Gujarati kitchen is complete without these essential recipes, and I highly recommend keeping most of them in your cupboard or fridge. It's worth noting that Gujaratis generally purchase the Coriander-cumin Powder and the Pickle Masala, and they can be found easily at Indian supermarkets.

These basic recipes make sufficient quantities for any dish in this book. The condiments in the next chapter will feed a family of four, with a little extra. Any leftovers can be stored as instructed in the recipes.

CORIANDER-CUMIN POWDER
DHANA-JEERU

GF   DF   VG   Q

Prep time: 5–10 minutes

75g/2¾oz/1 cup coriander seeds
25g/1oz/¼ cup cumin seeds

Heat a dry heavy-bottomed frying pan or skillet over a low heat. Add the cumin seeds and roast for 3–5 minutes. Turn the heat off and set aside to cool completely. Grind both coriander and cumin seeds in a blender until they become a smooth powder. Coriander-cumin powder can be stored in an airtight container for up to 3 months.

DHANA-JEERU: THE MAGIC POTION IN GUJARATI COOKING!

Dhana-jeeru powder is the hallmark of Gujarati cuisine, and no Gujarati home is without this quintessential ingredient. When roasted coriander and cumin seeds are ground together, a fragrant, lightly roasted powder is created that is a key addition to creating distinct Gujarati flavours. In fact, dhana-jeeru features in just about everything except sweet dishes, plain rice, Kadhi (page 125) and Roti (page 168).

Coriander and cumin are grown in the Unjha district of north Gujarat and harvested around the festival of Holi in the month of March. The seeds are bought separately, cleaned and dried under the hot sun. They may be very lightly roasted before being ground into a powder (the ratio is 3 parts coriander seeds to 1 part cumin seeds) and stored for the year.

What is so special about this dull greenish-yellow powder? Coriander has a citrusy-sweet mellow flavour that works well with cumin's slightly bitter taste and strong aroma and together they cook wonders! Dhana-jeeru blends well with any other masala (spice blend), adding to the overall taste of what is globally celebrated as spicy Indian cooking.

GREEN PASTE

GF   DF   VG   Q

Prep time: 5 minutes

Combine all the ingredients in a food processor or blender and blend to a smooth paste. It can be stored in an airtight container in the fridge for 5 days.

80g/2¾oz/2 cups chopped
  coriander (cilantro)
4–5 green chillies, stems removed
4–5 garlic cloves
salt, to taste
2–3 tbsp water

Basic Recipes

GARLIC PASTE

GF   DF   VG   Q

Prep time: 5 minutes

160g/5¾oz/1 cup garlic cloves
3–4 tbsp oil

Place the garlic in a blender or food processor and blitz for 1 minute, stopping after 30 seconds to scrape down the sides of the jug to ensure even blitzing. Add the oil and blitz for 3–5 minutes to a very smooth paste.

Store in an airtight container in the fridge for up to 3 days. See also the Freezer Storage Tip (page 32).

MY LOVE OF GARLIC PASTE

I love creating new dishes. I pay close attention to how a dish is unfolding before me but more importantly, I *respect* ingredients. If we prepare each ingredient with love and care, it will, in turn, deliver on flavour and texture: nurture the ingredients and they will nurture you.

And this is the relationship I have with one of my favourite ingredients: garlic. When a dish that features garlic is cooking in the kitchen, I am catapulted thirty years back in time – especially when the cook is using fresh garlic scapes, which are the green stalks that grow out of the bulb. Growing garlic at home is very easy. If you have a garden or a balcony, you need only the cloves and a pot. It is a low-maintenance vegetable and grows well throughout winter – not even the rain will halt its flourishing.

One of the most important condiments I couldn't wait to share is this simple yet extraordinary garlic paste. A well-made garlic paste surpasses chopped or minced garlic in flavour and texture and really enhances a dish. I use homemade garlic paste in the recipes throughout the book and I encourage you to do the same for optimal results and flavour.

The difference between other garlic pastes and mine is the texture: my garlic paste is very fine and smooth. It is also preservative-free, and not a lot is needed to pack a punch, so a batch will last a long time. I believe that my method does this superb ingredient the most justice and I know that if you try it, you will never prepare it any other way. This easy recipe will come in handy as I refer to it frequently throughout the book.

The aroma and flavour of garlic hold special nostalgia for me. It features in most of my Gujarati dishes and Amritsari Chole (page 143), an adaptation of the chickpea dish from the region of Amritsar itself, and I have been told that it's far superior to the local chole.

Not only is garlic an important part of my cooking for maximum flavour, but I enjoy knowing that it has so many health benefits. Garlic has been used throughout history for medicinal purposes and it's easy to see why: garlic is low in calories, low in saturated fat, low in sodium, and the active compounds in garlic have been known to reduce blood pressure. All this – and it's tasty! Step aside apples: a clove of garlic a day is all you need for good health.

GINGER PASTE

GF DF VG Q

Prep time: 5 minutes

150g/5½oz/1 cup ginger,
  peeled and cut into 2.5cm
  (1-inch) cubes

2–3 tbsp water (optional)

Place the ginger in a blender or food processor and blitz for 1 minute, stopping after 30 seconds to scrape down the sides of the jug to ensure even blitzing. Add water if needed and continue to blitz for 15–20 seconds until the mixture has a coarse consistency.

Store in an airtight container in the fridge for 3 days. See also the Freezer Storage Tip.

FREEZER STORAGE TIP

The garlic, ginger and the chilli pastes can be transferred into zip-top bags and the mixture flattened with a rolling pin before storing in the freezer. This will make it easier to cut and use as needed. Alternatively, for the garlic paste, you can portion it into small ice-cube trays (one teaspoon per compartment) and once frozen, transfer the portions into a zip-top bag. Garlic, ginger and chilli pastes can be stored in the freezer for up to a month.

GREEN CHILLI PASTE

GF DF VG Q

Prep time: 5 minutes

60g/2oz/1 cup green chillies,
  stems removed and cut into
  2.5cm (1-inch) segments

2–3 tbsp water (optional)

Place the chillies in a blender or food processor and blitz for 1 minute, stopping after 30 seconds to scrape down the sides of the jug to ensure even blitzing. Add water if needed and continue to blitz for 30–40 seconds until the mixture is coarse in consistency.

Store in an airtight container in the fridge for up to 4–5 days. See also Freezer Storage Tip above.

PICKLE MASALA

GF DF VG

Prep time: 5–10 minutes
+ 4–5 days marinating
Cook time: 15 minutes

Dry pickle masalas (methi masala or achar powder) of all kinds are a very important part of Indian cuisine. The pickle can be made from green mangoes, limes, fresh green and red chillies and mixed vegetables. The various pickle (or achar) masalas available in the north of India tend to include coarsely ground fenugreek seeds and mustard seeds, red chilli powder, asafoetida powder (hing) and salt. While I generally use store-bought pickle masala, here's a recipe if you're looking to make it at home.

90g/3¼oz/½ cup fenugreek seeds (methi kuria), crushed

34g/1¼oz/¼ cup split yellow mustard seeds (rai kuria)

1 tbsp salt

2 tsp asafoetida

3 tbsp groundnut (peanut) oil

25g/1oz/¼ cup Kashmiri chilli powder

1 tbsp red chilli powder

½ tsp citric acid

Put the fenugreek and mustard seeds in a dry heavy-bottomed frying pan or skillet and roast for 10 minutes over a low heat, while stirring continuously. Tip the seeds onto a plate and let them cool. Add the salt to the same pan and roast for 1–2 minutes, then set aside.

Transfer the roasted seeds to a blender or food processor and blitz for 6–8 seconds to a coarse consistency. Put the mixture in a bowl, make a well in the centre and add the asafoetida, but do not mix.

Heat the oil in a small saucepan over a medium heat until you begin to see smoke. Immediately pour the oil over the asafoetida and cover the bowl for 2–3 minutes.

Uncover, stir in the chilli powders and mix well. (The chilli powders are added after pouring in the oil in order to retain their colour.) Add the roasted salt and the citric acid and mix well again. Set aside for 4–5 days to marinate before use.

Note: Leftover pickle masala can be stored in an airtight glass jar for 6 months.

FENUGREEK SPROUTS
METHI SPROUTS

GF DF VG

Prep time: 5 minutes +
2 days soaking

90g/3¼oz/½ cup fenugreek seeds

Soak the seeds in a bowl of cold water for 8 hours. Drain well and place the seeds in a glass jar. Cover tightly using a lid that has holes, then set aside overnight. Add 1 tablespoon tepid water to the jar and set aside for another day or until there are 1cm (½-inch) visible sprouts. Use the sprouts as needed in the recipe. They can be stored in the fridge for up to 3 days.

CASHEW PASTE

GF DF VG Q

Prep time: 5 minutes +
30 minutes soaking

60g/2oz/½ cup cashew nuts
185ml/6fl oz/¾ cup hot water

Soak the cashew nuts in the hot water for 30 minutes. Transfer the mixture to a blender or food processor and blitz to a smooth paste, adding another 2–3 tablespoons water if needed.

Cashew paste can be stored in an airtight container in the fridge for 4–5 days.

TOMATO PURÉE

GF DF VG Q

Prep time: 5 minutes
Cook time: 10 minutes

240ml/8fl oz/1 cup water
4–5 ripe tomatoes

Bring the water to the boil in a saucepan. Add the tomatoes and cook over a medium-high heat for 10 minutes. Set aside to cool.

Peel the tomatoes, then transfer both the water and tomatoes to a blender and blend to a smooth paste. The purée can be stored in an airtight container in the fridge for up to 3 days.

TAMARIND PURÉE

GF DF VG

Prep time: 10 minutes +
1 hour soaking

750ml/26fl oz/3¼ cups hot water
160g/5¾oz/1 cup tamarind pulp

Bring the water to the boil in a small saucepan, then turn off the heat and soak the tamarind in the hot water for 1 hour, covering the pan. Using your hands, press the mixture through a sieve and discard the fibrous part.

Tamarind purée can be stored in an airtight container in the fridge for up to a week, or it can be frozen in a freezer-safe zip-top bag for up to 3 months. Thaw before using.

TAMARIND

Tamarind (imli, amli, puli) is a fruit of a tropical tree of the same name. The ripened fruit has a soft pulp that is sour, tart and tangy. It is high in nutrients, minerals and vitamin C.

Tamarind pulp is dried, salted and packed for use throughout the year. As and when required, a piece of the pulp is soaked for a while in some warm water. It is kneaded until a thick sauce remains and the fibrous part is discarded. The sauce, or purée, in different concentrations, can be added directly into curries, Gujarati dal and especially south Indian sambhars (stews) and rasams (soups) or when sweetened with grated jaggery, dates and roasted cumin powder, it becomes the 'sweet' chutney to go with samosas (see page 102) and tikkis (patties)!

STRAINED YOGURT

GF

Prep time: 5 minutes +
2 hours draining

860g/1lb 4oz/4 cups plain
    full-fat yogurt

Layer three sheets of paper towel on a large chopping board set over
a sink or large plate. Put the yogurt onto the paper-lined board and
place another three sheets of paper towel on top. Place a 3–4kg (6–8lb)
weight on top to weigh it down gently and set aside for 2 hours, until all
the water has drained. Scrape the yogurt from the towels and transfer to
a clean bowl.

Strained yogurt can be stored in an airtight container in the fridge for
up to 5 days.

CHUTNEYS & OTHER CONDIMENTS

BESAN CHUTNEY

GF   Q

Generally, chutney is made with fresh ingredients such as garlic or fresh herbs, but when those are not available, you can also use gram flour (besan). A besan chutney is always served with Methi na Gota (page 72) because of its unique flavour profile.

Serves 4
Prep time: 10 minutes
Cook time: 5 minutes

60g/2oz/½ cup gram flour (besan)

50g/1¾oz/¼ cup plain
   full-fat yogurt

1 tsp sugar

¼ tsp ground turmeric

salt, to taste

570ml/20fl oz/2½ cups water

1 tbsp oil

1 tsp mustard seeds

pinch of asafoetida

½ tsp cumin seeds

6–8 fresh curry leaves

1–2 green chillies, stems removed
   and sliced

3 tbsp chopped coriander
   (cilantro), to garnish

Methi na Gota (page 72), to serve

Put the gram flour, yogurt, sugar, turmeric and salt in a bowl and whisk well until there are no lumps. Add the water and whisk, again until there are no lumps. Set aside.

Heat the oil in a pan and add the mustard seeds. Once they begin to crackle, reduce the heat to low and add the asafoetida, cumin seeds and curry leaves. Gently fry for 5–6 seconds, before adding the gram flour mixture. Add the green chillies. Cook over a low heat for 4–5 minutes, stirring continuously to prevent lumps forming. The desired consistency should be that of a smooth, creamy soup, so do not allow the mixture to cook and reduce too quickly. Add up to another 125ml/4fl oz/½ cup water if it is too thick.

Garnish with the coriander and serve immediately with methi na gota.

Note: This chutney is best made fresh as the texture is compromised if made ahead of time and reheated.

GREEN GARLIC CHUTNEY

GF   DF   VG   Q

This traditional Gujarati recipe for chutney is so versatile: it can be used to accompany snacks (farsans) or can be part of a thali. But take note: a little goes a long way!

Makes 215g/7½oz/¾ cup
Prep time: 5 minutes

120g/4¼oz/3 cups chopped coriander (cilantro)

75g/2¾oz/¾ cup chopped garlic scapes or 3 garlic cloves

2 green chillies, stems removed

salt, to taste

Place all the ingredients in a blender and blitz to a smooth paste. Add 2–3 tablespoons water if needed.

Green garlic chutney can be stored in an airtight container in the fridge for up to 5 days. You can make a larger batch by doubling the quantity – it also stores well in a zip-top bag in the freezer.

MINT CHUTNEY

GF   DF   VG   Q

This simple, easy chutney is not something that is served all the time in Indian cuisine, but it makes for a vibrant, refreshing accompaniment for Crispy Samosas (page 102).

Makes about 290g/10¼oz/1 cup
Prep time: 5 minutes

1 tsp cumin seeds

3 garlic cloves

40g/1½oz/1 cup chopped
   coriander (cilantro)

50g/1¾oz/2 cups chopped
   mint leaves

1 tbsp fresh lime juice

2–3 green chillies, stems removed

salt, to taste

Heat a small dry pan and add the cumin seeds. Toast over a medium heat for 2–4 minutes. Tip onto a plate and allow to cool. Place all the ingredients in a blender and blitz to a smooth paste. Add 2–3 tablespoons water if needed.

Mint chutney can be stored in an airtight container in the fridge for up to 1 week. You can make a larger batch by doubling the quantity – it also stores well in a zip-top bag in the freezer.

PEANUT CHUTNEY

GF · DF · VG · Q

It was love at first taste when I discovered this easy and simple peanut chutney at a friend's house nearly twenty years ago, and I still enjoy it as much today. I always have a batch of it in my freezer for my family.

Makes about 290g/10¼oz/1 cup
Prep time: 10 minutes
Cook time: 5 minutes

5 tsp oil

2 garlic cloves

4 dried red chillies

135g/4¾oz/1 cup roasted peanuts (see Note)

125ml/4fl oz/½ cup water

¾ tsp mustard seeds

¾ tsp cumin seeds

5–7 fresh curry leaves

Heat 2 teaspoons of the oil in a small pan over a low heat and add the garlic and 2 dried chillies. Cook for 2–3 minutes until the garlic and chillies are roasted and turn light brown in colour. Remove from the heat.

Place the peanuts, the roasted garlic and chillies and the water in a blender and blitz to a smooth paste. Set aside.

Heat the remaining 3 teaspoons of oil in a clean pan and add the mustard seeds. Once they begin to crackle, add the cumin seeds, curry leaves and remaining dried chillies. Stir and cook for 4–5 seconds, then immediately pour over the peanut paste and mix well.

Peanut chutney can be stored in an airtight container in the fridge for up to 4 days.

Note: Store-bought roasted peanuts are salted, but if you are roasting and peeling your own peanuts, you may need to add a pinch of salt to the mixture.

CURRY LEAF CHUTNEY

GF   DF   VG   Q

My older sister-in-law prepares this recipe using a pestle and mortar, and quite honestly I could eat this straight from the bowl – it's that good! For the sake of time, I've provided a simpler recipe using a blender or food processor. You can buy curry leaves in Asian supermarkets.

Makes about 150g/5½oz/½ cup
Prep time: 10 minutes

50g/1¾oz/2 cups fresh curry leaves

2–3 green chillies, stems removed

1 tbsp desiccated (dried shredded) or grated fresh coconut

1 tbsp sesame seeds

2 tbsp roasted peanuts

salt, to taste

2½ tbsp groundnut (peanut) oil

3 tbsp water

Place all the ingredients, apart from the oil and water, in a blender or food processor and blend for 3–4 minutes to a coarse texture, stopping occasionally to scrape the sides of the bowl. Add the oil and water and blitz for another 1–2 minutes. The chutney should have a coarse pesto-like consistency and not be a smooth paste.

Fresh curry leaf chutney can be stored in an airtight container in the fridge for up to a week. You can make a larger batch by doubling the quantity – it also stores well in a zip-top bag in the freezer.

Chutneys & Other Condiments

SWEET TAMARIND CHUTNEY

 GF   DF   VG   Q

This delicious sweet-and-sour sauce pairs beautifully with some of Gujarat's most popular appetizers and chaat dishes. I absolutely cannot get enough of it, so I prepare it in large batches to ensure it's always on hand. Trust me, once you make this, you'll never buy store-bought tamarind chutney again.

Makes 290g/10¼oz/1 cup
Prep time: 5–10 minutes
Cook time: 5 minutes

1 tsp cumin seeds

125g/4½oz/½ cup Tamarind Purée (page 36)

120ml/4fl oz/½ cup water

½ tsp chilli powder

1 tsp chaat powder

½ tsp salt

200g/7oz/1 cup brown sugar or roughly chopped jaggery (gur), plus extra to taste

Heat a small dry pan and add the cumin seeds. Toast over a medium heat for 2–4 minutes. Tip onto a plate and allow to cool.

Place the tamarind purée, water, toasted cumin seeds, chilli powder, chaat powder, salt and brown sugar (or jaggery) in a blender and blitz for 2 minutes. Taste and adjust to your desired sweetness.

Tamarind chutney can be stored in an airtight container in the fridge for up to 5 days. You can make a larger batch by doubling the quantity – it also stores well in a zip-top bag in the freezer.

QUICK AND EASY MANGO PICKLE

METHIA KERI

GF ▸ DF ▸ VG ▸ Q

Makes about 250g/9oz/2½ cups
Prep time: 5 minutes
Cook time: 5 minutes

2 tbsp oil

1 tsp mustard seeds

¼ tsp asafoetida

¼ tsp ground turmeric

6 tbsp Pickle Masala (page 34),
   or use store-bought

2 unripe mangoes, peeled and
   cut into thin wedges or 2.5cm
   (1-inch) cubes (see Note)

Parathas (page 174) or Bhakhri
   (page 166), to serve

Also known as mango achar, this pickle is served with many of the recipes throughout the book. What makes it so appealing is how deceptively easy and quick it is to make – all you need is 10 minutes to create an authentic pickle to serve with just about anything. Store-bought pickle masala works well for this recipe if you don't have time to make your own – just check that it's not laden with preservatives.

Heat the oil in a small pan and add the mustard seeds. Once they begin to crackle, remove the pan from the heat, add the asafoetida and the ground turmeric and mix well. Add the pickle masala, then mix well again. Combine the mixture with the mangoes, then serve at room temperature with parathas or bhakhri.

Mango pickle can be stored in an airtight container in the fridge for up to 3 days.

Note: It's important to select mangoes at the right stage of ripeness: here you do not want ripe mango because it will not hold the texture and it will be too sweet. Choose ones that are raw, firm or slightly soft.

MANGO AND RED ONION KACHUMBER

GF   DF   VG   Q

This tasty condiment is the Gujarati version of a mango salsa. Refreshingly sweet with a mild heat, kachumber is traditionally served as part of the thali (page 106), but it can also be served with Roti (page 168), Bhakhri (page 166) or Yellow Rice (page 184).

Makes about 200g/7oz/2 cups
Prep time: 5 minutes +
30 minutes standing

1 mango, finely chopped

1 red onion, finely chopped

1 tsp ground cumin

½ tsp red chilli powder

2½ tsp sugar

¾ tsp salt, or to taste

½ tsp fresh lime juice

Combine all the ingredients in a small bowl and mix well for 1–2 minutes, then set aside for 30 minutes. It can be served at room temperature or stored in an airtight container in the fridge for 1–2 days.

Note: It's important to select mangoes at the right stage of ripeness: here you do not want ripe mango because it will not hold the texture and it will be too sweet. Choose ones that are raw, firm or slightly soft.

SALADS & RAITAS

GREEN CHICKPEA SALAD

GF   DF   VG

Green chickpeas (chana) are little buttery, vibrantly coloured legumes. They grow in fuzzy pods on vines and can be retrieved by simply opening the pods and picking them out. They are a popular ingredient in Gujarati cooking and I simply adore them!

I was reminded of green chickpeas when enjoying a salad, similar to this one, at a friend's home. I fondly remembered eating them as a child, and memories of my mom roasting them in an Indian wok (kadai) came flooding back to me. They are high in fibre and can be enjoyed as a healthy snack when roasted and served with a squeeze of lime and a pinch of salt. Here, they feature in a fresh and zingy salad, which I know you will love.

Serves 2
Prep time: 10 minutes
Cook time: 40–50 minutes

350g/12oz/6 cups fresh chickpeas or 150g/5½oz/1 cup frozen green chickpeas (leela chana)

2 small yellow squash or patty pan squash, cut into 2.5cm (1-inch) dice

2 small tomatoes, chopped

30g/1oz/¼ cup finely chopped red onion

1 tbsp fresh lime juice

2 tbsp chopped mint leaves (optional)

1–2 small green chillies, stems removed and finely grated

¼ tsp freshly ground black pepper

salt, to taste

If using frozen green chickpeas, place them in a colander and run hot water briefly over them. Drain well. Place them in a microwave-safe bowl and cook on high for 3–4 minutes until tender.

If using fresh chickpeas, heat a dry heavy-bottomed frying pan or skillet over a low heat and roast them for 40–50 minutes, while stirring regularly, until browned. Allow to cool. Open the pods and gently push the chickpeas out with your fingers.

Combine the chickpeas, squash, tomato and onion in a bowl. Stir in the lime juice, mint, if using, and chilli and season with the black pepper and salt.

Salads & Raitas

GREEN GRAPE AND TOMATO SALAD

GF   DF   VG   Q

I have my eldest sister (a talented cook) to thank for this salad. Grapes are not typical in Indian recipes but they lend a sweetness that is delicious combined with tomatoes, especially with the addition of cumin.

Serves 4
Prep time: 5 minutes

Simply combine all the ingredients in a serving bowl and toss gently to evenly coat. Serve at once or cover and refrigerate immediately until ready to serve. Bring back to room temperature before serving.

150g/5½oz/1 cup green grapes, cut in half

170g/6oz/1 cup red or yellow cherry tomatoes, cut in half

40–80g/1½–2¾oz/¼–½ cup fresh pomegranate seeds (optional)

2 tsp fresh lime juice

2 tsp toasted cumin seeds, coarsely crushed

1 tbsp sugar

1 tsp salt, or to taste

YOGURT RAITA

GF Q

Yogurt raita with a magical twist – just a little sugar can bring an unassuming raita to life. I spent hours and hours refining my raita recipe. It was a lot of work, but this version grabs the attention of my son and is very close to my heart.

To those of you who have reached out to me after having tasted it at one of my dinner parties, thank you!

Serves 4
Prep time: 5 minutes
Cook time: 5 minutes

430g/15¼oz/2 cups plain full-fat yogurt

5 tbsp water

60g/2oz/½ cup chopped red onion

40g/1½oz/¼ cup chopped tomato

2½ tsp sugar

½ tsp salt, or to taste

1½ tbsp oil

1 tsp mustard seeds

3–4 dried red chillies

8–10 fresh curry leaves

Parathas (page 174) or Dhebras (page 172), to serve

Whisk the yogurt and water in a large bowl until smooth. Add the red onion, tomato, sugar and salt. Mix well and set aside.

Heat the oil in a small pan over a medium heat and add the mustard seeds. Once they begin to crackle, add the dried chillies and curry leaves. Mix and sauté for 4–6 seconds, then immediately pour the hot seasoning over the whisked yogurt and mix well.

Serve with parathas or dhebras.

PAPADUM SALAD

GF DF VG Q

Simple and elegant with deliciously fresh flavours, this appetizer was a must when I returned home from a trip to Rajasthan in the north of India. I now serve this often and love the contrast of salad and crispy cone. These must be served soon after assembling, otherwise the toasted papadums turn soggy.

It's worth noting that mung bean sprouts are smaller and shorter than the regular sprouts you might find at the supermarket. They can be purchased fresh at Indian food markets, or you can make them at home by following the Fenugreek Sprouts recipe on page 35. Soak 110g/3¾oz/½ cup mung beans in 240ml/8fl oz/1 cup water.

Serves 4
Prep time: 10 minutes

4 plain papadums

30g/1oz/½ cup beansprouts (mung bean sprouts)

40g/1½oz/¼ cup finely chopped tomato

30g/1oz/¼ cup chopped red onion

8 mint leaves, finely chopped

1 tbsp finely chopped coriander (cilantro), plus extra to garnish

2 tsp fresh lime juice

½ tsp Coriander-cumin Powder (page 29) or chaat powder

salt, to taste

Use a sharp knife or pizza cutter to cut each papadum in half. Place the papadum halves one at a time into a hot toaster oven for 10 seconds or until small bumps appear over the surface. (Alternatively, preheat a large frying pan on a medium-high heat and heat the papadum for 10 seconds on one side.)

Working quickly, using oven gloves, fold each half into a cone shape by joining the two sides (curved-end up) at an angle. It is essential that this is done while the papadum is still hot. Set aside to cool and set into shape. Repeat with the remaining papadum halves.

In a bowl, combine the beansprouts, tomato, red onion, mint, coriander, lime juice and coriander-cumin powder or chaat powder. Season with salt and mix well.

Fill each cone with 1–2 tablespoons of filling. Garnish with chopped coriander and serve immediately.

SUNSET BEETROOT SALAD

GF   DF   VG

Serves 4
Prep time: 10 minutes
+ 1 hour standing
Cook time: 45–60 minutes

Fresh, beautifully coloured beetroots (beets) take centre stage in this refreshingly light summer salad, which conceals an unexpected heap of peppery rocket (arugula). I do like the element of surprise. This was inspired by a dish I ate in Sydney, Australia, and I'm so grateful that the chef gave us a tour of his grand kitchen and shared the recipe for this bright golden dish.

4 golden beetroots (beets)

For the dressing
1 large shallot, minced

2 garlic cloves, minced

60ml/2fl oz/¼ cup red wine vinegar

¼ tsp coarse sea salt (kosher salt)

1 tbsp sugar

60ml/2fl oz/¼ cup extra-virgin olive oil

To serve
100g/3½oz/4 cups rocket (arugula) leaves or spring leaves/greens, chopped

4 tbsp salted and roasted pistachio nuts, shelled

Preheat the oven to 200°C fan/220°C/425°F/gas mark 7.

In a small bowl, combine the shallot, garlic, vinegar, salt and sugar and set aside for 1 hour.

Meanwhile, wrap the beetroots in foil and seal tightly. Roast on the middle shelf of the oven for 45–60 minutes. Set aside to cool.

Peel and slice the beetroots into thin medallions. Set aside.

In a bowl, combine the rocket and pistachios. Add the oil to the dressing and whisk well. Drizzle 4–5 tablespoons of the dressing over the salad and toss well. (Leftover dressing can be stored in a glass jar in the fridge for up to a week.)

Divide the salad equally between 4 plates. Arrange a beetroot medallion on top of each portion of salad, then overlap more medallions around it. Serve immediately.

SPINACH CHAAT
PALAK PATTA CHAAT

GF   Q

Serves 4
Prep time: 15 minutes
Cook time: 15 minutes

Experiencing the culinary culture at every destination I visit fuels my love for cooking. Indian cookery is full of interesting and complex flavours – take this super-tasty chaat made with baby spinach. Despite being deep-fried, it's a surprisingly light meal and I am only sorry that I didn't discover this recipe sooner.

For the sweet yogurt sauce
110g/3¾oz/½ cup plain full-fat yogurt

½ tsp ground cumin

¼ tsp chaat powder

1 tbsp brown sugar

pinch of salt

For the spinach chaat
95g/3¼oz/¾ cup gram flour (besan)

2 tbsp rice flour

2 tsp chaat powder

¼ tsp chilli powder

¼ tsp salt

185ml/6fl oz/¾ cup water

700–950ml/24–32fl oz/3–4 cups oil, for deep-frying

115g/4oz fresh baby spinach leaves, washed and patted dry

Sweet Tamarind Chutney (page 45)

To garnish
30g/1oz/¼ cup finely chopped red onion

a few cherry tomatoes, halved

75g/2¾oz/½ cup fresh pomegranate seeds (optional)

For the sweet yogurt sauce, simply whisk together all the ingredients with 3 tablespoons water. Set aside.

For the spinach chaat, combine the gram flour, rice flour, chaat powder, chilli powder, salt and 60ml/2fl oz/¼ cup of the water in a bowl and whisk. Now add the remaining 125ml/4fl oz/½ cup water and whisk the batter until smooth and free of lumps.

Heat the oil, about 7.5cm (3 inches) deep, in a wok or deep saucepan over a medium-high heat. (Test the heat with a small drop of batter: if it falls to the bottom and pops up gradually, the oil is perfect; if the batter rises and browns too quickly, the oil is too hot; and if the batter sinks and doesn't rise, the oil is not hot enough.) Working in small batches to avoid overcrowding, dip the spinach leaves in the batter, then carefully lower the battered leaves into the pan in a single layer to cover the entire surface. (Be careful: the water content in the spinach may cause spattering.) Deep-fry for 2–3 minutes, using the spoon or skimmer to move the leaves around to prevent them from sticking together. Using the same tool, transfer the spinach to a paper towel-lined plate to drain.

Repeat the process until all the leaves are fried, ensuring that the oil temperature is maintained at all times.

Transfer the deep-fried spinach to a four plates. Drizzle 2 tablespoons each of sweet yogurt sauce and tamarind chutney over each plate. Garnish with the red onion, tomatoes and pomegranate seeds, if using. Serve immediately before the spinach becomes soggy.

APPETIZERS

FARSANS

For one of the best culinary experiences of any modern town or city, you can do no better than to follow the locals' lead and seek out its street food. Throughout the world, humble roadside stalls are a glorious tradition that has endured despite globalization. With cultural exchange over time, some of the gastronomic delicacies they offer may have become 'fusion food' but these stalls provide a unique experience of the culinary heritage. And in Gujarat the diversity of snacks, or farsans, sold as street food is simply unbeatable. They are always accompanied with fried green chillies and a green coriander chilli or garlic-red chutney.

Many Gujarati street foods are deep-fried or fried and MUST be eaten straight from the heat of the cast-iron pan known as a kadai or tawa. Usually they come with a piping-hot cup of slightly milky, fresh ginger- and masala-spiced tea. The two most popular street foods are Bhajiyas (pages 69 and 84) – deep-fried fritters of chopped vegetables (bhaji means fried vegetables) dipped in a spiced batter made from various types of flour – and dals, often mixed with finely cut fresh leaf veggies, such as spinach and fenugreek, and green chillies, ginger and garlic.

Dakor na Gota (page 75) – ball-shaped bhajiyas with a particular spice mix – are a speciality of Gujarat. They take their name from the temple in the small city of Dakor, which is a popular Vaishanav pilgrimage destination visited by thousands of worshippers every full moon in the Hindu lunar calendar. The fritter batter from Dakor has become hugely popular.

Other flour-based Gujarati farsans are steamed, not fried, to make them soft and spongy. They include Khaman (page 77), the similar surti locho from Surat, Palak na Muthiya (page 91), Khandvi (page 66) and Papdi no Lot (page 78). They are often mixed with protein-rich legumes and vegetables.

Coming from a grain merchant family (my father was a manufacturer of a besan-processing mill), I came to appreciate the value of besan (chickpea/gram flour) from an early age. My dear father was particular about the quality of besan and would hire a small snack-stall owner across from his mill to make fresh farsans from the besan in front of him so he could taste-test every batch produced. It's no wonder I became such a passionate ambassador for the quality of ingredients.

The recipes in this chapter display a clever combination of spices, giving uniquely subtle and exotic end results. This, and the fact that Gujaratis have perfected the balance of sweet, sour and spicy in every bite, means that, for me, farsans are undoubtedly superior to the snacks and appetizers from any other region of India. Here I have included twenty-five high-protein, lip-smacking appetizers, which form an integral part of Gujarati feasting.

CHICKPEA ROLLS

KHANDVI

GF   Q

My dear aunt taught me to make chickpea rolls when I was a little girl. This melt-in-the-mouth snack is popular not only with Gujaratis but all Indian food-lovers. It requires a degree of effort and patience, but once mastered you will do it again and again.

Serves 3
Prep time: 20 minutes
Cook time: 10–15 minutes

For the rolls
oil or cooking spray, for greasing

125g/4½oz/1 cup gram flour (besan)

110g/3¾oz/½ cup plain full-fat yogurt

350ml/12fl oz/1½ cups water

¾ tsp ground turmeric

salt, to taste

For the seasoning
2 tbsp oil

2 tsp mustard seeds

pinch of asafoetida

6 Thai green chillies or 2 tbsp sliced green chillies

2 dried red chillies (optional)

2 tsp sesame seeds

To garnish (optional)
2 tbsp fresh or frozen grated coconut

1 tbsp chopped coriander (cilantro)

Grease 4–5 dinner plates with oil or cooking spray.

Combine the gram flour and yogurt in a large bowl and whisk until smooth. Add the water and whisk well. Add the ground turmeric and salt and mix well to make a smooth batter. Transfer the mixture to a frying pan or skillet and cook for 12 minutes over a low-medium heat, stirring continuously until thickened.

Working quickly while the batter is still hot, divide the cooked batter between the oiled plates. Using a large stainless-steel serving spoon, spread the mixture out in a thin, even layer. Allow to cool for 5–7 minutes.

Cut into strips about 5cm (2 inches) wide and roll up. You should be able to make about 15–20 rolls.

Next, make the seasoning. Heat the oil in a small frying pan or skillet and add the mustard seeds. Once they begin to crackle, add the asafoetida, chillies and sesame seeds and heat through for a few seconds over a medium heat.

Pour the seasoning over the rolls and toss gently to coat. Garnish with the grated coconut and coriander, if using.

ADZUKI BEAN PATTIES

GF   DF   VG

This tasty vegetarian dish is great either for breakfast or any time of the day! Adzuki or aduki beans, also known as red chori beans, are high in protein, promoting a feeling of fullness and making them an ideal option to incorporate into your morning routine. Half a cup (100g/3½oz) of cooked beans provides 48g (1¾oz) of protein. The dish requires only soaking time, which can also be done the night before, and the rest can be whipped up effortlessly. You will be pleasantly surprised at the fantastic flavours of these patties, even though they boast such a relatively short list of ingredients.

Serves 4–5
Prep time: 10 minutes +
6–8 hours soaking
Cook time: 15–25 minutes

360g/12¾oz/2 cups dried adzuki beans (red chori beans)

700ml/24fl oz/3 cups cold water, plus 1–2 tbsp as needed

5cm (2-inch) piece of fresh ginger, peeled

3–4 green chillies, stems removed

1½ tsp cumin seeds

10–15 fresh curry leaves

salt, to taste

oil, for frying

Curry Leaf Chutney (page 44) or Green Garlic Chutney (page 41), to serve

Wash and soak the beans in the water overnight or for 6–8 hours. Combine the ginger, chillies, cumin seeds, curry leaves and salt in a blender or food processor and blitz for 2 minutes to a coarse consistency. Now add the soaked beans (along with the soaking water) and blitz for 30–40 seconds, stopping halfway to scrape down the sides of the jug/bowl to ensure an even consistency. Add 4 tablespoons of water, if needed. Transfer the mixture to a small bowl and mix well.

Heat a little oil in a frying pan or skillet over a medium heat. Ladle 3 tablespoons of batter into the pan to create a patty. Make two more and fry for 2–4 minutes per side, until golden brown. (Depending on the size of your pan, you may need to do them in batches of three, adding a little more oil before cooking each batch.)

Serve warm with chutney.

Appetizers

DEEP-FRIED POTATOES
BATATA NA BHAJIYA

GF   DF   VG   Q

Serves 4
Prep time: 15 minutes
Cook time: 5 minutes

125g/4½oz/1 cup gram flour (besan)

2 tbsp rice flour

150ml/5fl oz/½ cup plus 2 tbsp warm water

1 tsp chilli powder, plus extra for sprinkling

1 tsp Coriander-cumin Powder (page 29)

½ tsp sugar

½ tsp ajwain (carom) seeds

¼ tsp ground turmeric

700–950ml/24–32fl oz/3–4 cups oil, for deep-frying

1 large long potato, thinly sliced on a mandoline (you need 12–15 slices)

30g/1oz/¼ cup finely sliced red onion

salt, to taste

Teatime at weekends is incomplete without this delicious dish. In fact, they are an all-time favourite snack wherever we go – even on holiday! I carry the ingredients with me, and since we always stay in accommodation that includes a kitchen, I can simply pop to a local store to buy potatoes, then make Batata na Bhajiya for the family to ensure wherever we find ourselves always feels 'like home'. It's a simple recipe that features a crispy crust and a soft, melt-in-the-mouth centre. Perfect comfort food!

Whisk the gram flour, rice flour and warm water in a bowl for a minute. Add the chilli powder, coriander-cumin powder, sugar, ajwain seeds and turmeric and whisk until smooth.

Heat the oil in a deep saucepan over a medium–high heat. Dip the potato slices briefly in the batter. Working in batches to avoid overcrowding, carefully lower 2–3 at a time into the hot oil and fry for 10–12 seconds on each side (flipping once) until golden brown. Using a slotted spoon or skimmer, transfer to a tray lined with paper towels and set aside to drain.

In a small bowl, combine the red onion, some salt and a sprinkling of chilli powder and mix well. Serve alongside the potatoes.

CORN FRITTERS

GF   DF

I firmly believe good homemade garlic paste is the secret 'weapon' in many of my recipes as it boosts the flavour. Here, I have paired it with sweetcorn to enhance what I believe to be the world's greatest appetizer. Corn is a common ingredient in a Gujarati household and is very versatile.

To remove the kernels from the cob, trim the stalk end flat, stand the cob upright and slice off the kernels with a sharp knife before washing and draining them well. If you are using frozen corn kernels, thaw them before using.

Serves 4
Prep time: 10 minutes
Cook time: 25 minutes

550g/1lb 4oz/4 cups sweetcorn (corn), thawed if frozen

65g/2¼oz/½ cup finely chopped celery

50g/1¾oz/½ cup chopped spring onions (scallions)

2 red pearl onions, thinly sliced (optional)

1 tsp Garlic Paste (page 31)

70g/2½oz/½ cup plain (all-purpose) flour or rice flour

salt, to taste

½ tsp freshly ground black pepper

2 eggs, whisked

700–950ml/24–32fl oz/3–4 cups oil, for greasing and deep-frying

Combine the corn, celery, spring onions, red onion, if using, garlic paste, flour, salt and black pepper in a large bowl. Combine well and tip in the whisked eggs. Mix well.

Heat the oil in a deep saucepan over a medium heat. Brush a large metal slotted spoon with oil and drop 3–4 tablespoons of the mixture onto the spoon to form a patty. Carefully lower the batter-laden spoon into the hot oil and fry the fritter for 3 minutes. Using a butter knife to loosen the fritter, transfer it onto a tray lined with paper towels to drain the excess oil. Repeat the process with the remaining batter (you should make about 8 fritters), oiling the slotted spoon before frying each fritter.

Appetizers

BESAN AND FENUGREEK FRITTERS

METHI NA GOTA

DF VG

About two years ago, we went on a road trip to Mount Abu in north India's Rajasthan state. Up early one morning and craving chai and a typical Gujarati breakfast, we stopped at a small chain restaurant near Ahmedabad. Imagine our delight when the server came with a gourmet-looking bhajiya plate featuring methi na gota. They were so fluffy and melt-in-the-mouth, it took all my willpower not to ask for the recipe (which of course I eventually did). The server gave me a few clues about what went into them, but the rest was up to me to figure out on my return home. The recipe below is my interpretation and I think I did a pretty good job, as this is now very popular among my friends. I even taught my husband how to make them and it turns out he does an even better job than I do!

Serves 4–5
Prep time: 10 minutes +
15 minutes standing
Cook time: 10 minutes

250g/9oz/2 cups gram
   flour (besan)

½ bunch fresh fenugreek leaves
   (methi), picked and chopped
   (about 35g/1¼oz/1 cup)

2 tbsp coarse semolina (sooji)

1–2 green chillies, stems removed
   and thinly sliced

1 tbsp sugar

½ tsp bicarbonate of soda
   (baking soda)

pinch of Eno (fruit salt)

2 tbsp oil, warmed, plus
   700–950ml/24–32fl oz/
   3–4 cups for deep-frying

salt, to taste

240ml/8fl oz/1 cup water

Besan Chutney (page 40), to serve

In a large bowl, combine all the ingredients, except the oil for deep-frying, and whisk for 2 minutes until smooth, then cover and set aside for 15 minutes. Add another 1 tablespoon water to loosen the batter, and mix well.

Heat the cooking oil in a deep saucepan over a medium heat. Using a spoon, scoop 1½–2 tablespoons of batter and carefully drop it into the hot oil – the batter needs to be dropped from about 2.5cm/1 inch above the oil, so do be careful to avoid splatters. Reduce the heat to medium-low and deep-fry for 1½–2 minutes until very light golden all over. Remove with a slotted spoon and drain on a tray lined with paper towels. Repeat until all the batter is used up.

Serve with besan chutney.

Appetizers

DAKOR NA GOTA

GF DF VG

Serves 4
Prep time: 20 minutes + 2 hours
soaking + 15 minutes standing
Cook time: 10 minutes

Dakor na gota is a traditional Gujarati snack, originating from the religious centre of Dakor. I associate this snack with a feast eaten after prayers and offerings to the lord Krishna. These were trips taken with my beloved grandparents and, on the way, we always stopped at a roadside restaurant for gota and chai, where the chef would prepare the batter in front of us. This recipe came directly from the street vendor, so you are unlikely to find anything more authentic.

180g/6¼oz/1 cup dried split
   chickpeas (chana dal)

350ml/12fl oz/1½ cups water

2.5cm (1-inch) piece of fresh
   ginger, peeled

2–3 green chillies, stems removed,
   plus extra to garnish (optional)

1 tsp fennel seeds

1 tsp coriander seeds

1 tsp black peppercorns,
   slightly crushed

½ tsp ground turmeric

1 tsp chilli powder

½ tsp garam masala

¼ tsp bicarbonate of soda
   (baking soda)

2 tsp sugar

½ tsp fresh lime juice or Tamarind
   Purée (page 36)

salt, to taste

2 tsp oil, plus 700–950ml/24–
   32fl oz/3–4 cups for deep-frying

2 tbsp gram flour (besan)
   (optional)

Rinse, then soak the split chickpeas in a bowl with the water for 2 hours.

Combine the ginger and chillies in a blender or food processor and grind for 1–2 minutes to a coarse consistency, stopping to scrape down the sides occasionally. Drain the split chickpeas, then add them to the blender and blend for 20–30 seconds, retaining a coarse consistency.

Transfer the mixture to a mixing bowl and add the fennel seeds, coriander seeds, black peppercorns, ground turmeric, chilli powder, garam masala, bicarbonate of soda, sugar, lime juice or tamarind purée, salt and the 2 teaspoons of oil. Mix well, then cover and set aside for 15 minutes. The batter should have a good 'drop' consistency – if needed, add the gram flour.

Heat the oil in a deep saucepan over a medium heat. Using a spoon, carefully drop small portions (approximately 2 teaspoons) of the batter into the oil and fry for 1–2 minutes, turning them constantly until they are evenly browned on all sides. Turn the heat to medium-low. Using a slotted spoon or skimmer, transfer to a plate lined with paper towels to drain. Repeat until all the batter is used up.

Garnish with chillies, if liked.

YELLOW SPONGES

NYLON KHAMAN

GF

Serves 4
Prep time: 20 minutes +
20 minutes standing
Cook time: 20 minutes

For the yellow sponges

125g/4½oz/1 cup gram flour (besan)

1 tbsp icing (powdered) sugar

1 tbsp oil, plus extra for greasing

½ tsp citric acid

½ tsp salt

½ tsp bicarbonate of soda
(baking soda)

For the khaman chutney

1–2 small green chillies

4 squares yellow sponge (see above)

40g/1½oz/1 cup roughly chopped
coriander (cilantro)

2 tbsp plain full-fat yogurt

2 tsp sugar

For the seasoning

2 green chillies

3 tbsp oil

1 tbsp plus 1 tsp mustard seeds

¼ tsp asafoetida

1 tbsp sugar

To garnish (optional)

2 tbsp roughly chopped coriander
(cilantro)

1 tbsp grated fresh coconut

When you talk about Gujarat and its cuisine, the single most recognizable dish is khaman. I learnt how to make this delicious dish from a shop owner at a farsan mart. Nylon (meaning 'very soft' in Gujarati) khaman requires a little skill and practice to get the right texture and taste; I tested this dish about twenty times.

To make the yellow sponges, sift the gram flour into a medium bowl. Stir in 175ml/6fl oz/¾ cup warm water, the icing sugar, oil, citric acid and salt. Whisk for 2 minutes until smooth and free of lumps. Set aside for 15 minutes.

Bring some water to a simmer in a wok or large frying pan or skillet over a medium heat. Place a 5cm (2-inch) steamer rack in the centre of the wok and place a greased heatproof or stainless-steel 20cm (8-inch) plate or cake tin (baking pan), about 5cm (2 inches) deep, on top – we use a thali. Cover and heat until steam escapes through the lid.

Add the bicarbonate of soda to the batter and whisk vigorously, until the batter has doubled in size and becomes foamy. Immediately pour the batter onto the plate, then cover and cook for 15 minutes. The sponge is cooked when a cake tester (or fork) inserted in the centre comes out clean. Remove the plate immediately from the steamer and set aside to cool. Cut into 4cm (1½-inch) squares.

For the chutney, remove the stems from the chillies and place all the ingredients in a blender or food processor with 125ml/4fl oz/½ cup water and some salt to taste. Blend to a coarse paste.

For the seasoning, remove the stems from the chillies, and slice. Heat the oil in a small pan over a medium-low heat. Add the mustard seeds and fry until they begin to crackle, then add the asafoetida and chillies and cook for 4–6 seconds. Add the sugar and 2–3 tablespoons water, reduce the heat to low, and cook for 2 minutes. Pour the seasoning over the yellow sponges and leave for 3–5 minutes so the sugar water is absorbed.

Garnish the squares with the coriander and coconut, if using, then serve with the khaman chutney.

STEAMED RICE FLOUR
PAPDI NO LOT OR KHICHU

GF   DF   VG   Q

Early in my marriage, my husband enquired whether I knew how to make papdi no lot. I didn't. He vaguely recalled his mother's recipe and the two of us pieced together the elements. That same day, he invited Gujarati friends to our home, and we offered them some leftover papdi no lot from our trial batch. They loved it – and while I can't claim that I introduced them to this dish, I certainly brought back great memories of it for them.

Papdi no lot (also known as khichu) became a bit of an accidental success in our home as well. My kids – hooked on American food as many kids are – were simply uninterested in trying it every time I made it. Until one day, leftovers of this dish were all that was available to them. Being as hungry as they were, they had no choice but to start picking at it. Well, they devoured it all and now they love it! My favourite part of the story is that they could never remember the traditional name and simply called it 'Squishy Stuff' – so the name stuck. Oh, how it warms my heart when I get a text from my adult children asking if there is 'Squishy Stuff' at home…

Serves 5
Prep time: 10 minutes
Cook time: 15 minutes

2 tbsp oil, plus extra for oiling

1½ tsp cumin seeds

700ml/24fl oz/3 cups water

2 tbsp finely grated green chilli

1½ tsp salt, or to taste

140g/5oz/1 cup rice flour or brown rice flour

To serve
8–10 tsp olive or groundnut (peanut) oil

4 tsp Pickle Masala (page 34) (optional)

Heat the oil in a saucepan over a medium heat and add the cumin seeds. Once they begin to crackle, add the water, increase the heat to medium-high and boil for 5 minutes. Stir in the chilli and salt and boil for another 4 minutes.

Reduce the heat to low and stir in the rice flour in a fast, circular motion using the handle of a wooden spoon. The batter should be completely smooth with no lumps. Cover the pan with a lid and steam for 4–5 minutes. Set aside until cool enough to handle.

With slightly oiled hands, divide the dough into 5 equal pieces and shape each into a patty. Using your thumb, dent the centre. Pour 2 teaspoons of the olive or groundnut oil into the centre of each patty and top with pickle masala, if liked.

Appetizers

WHITE DHOKLA
SOOJI DHOKLA

This is the perfect snack for spontaneous hosting. Dhokla is a steamed sponge made with yogurt and coarse semolina (sooji). I've created my own version of this popular Gujarati dish, and it is so easy to make at home. If it proves tricky to find coarse semolina, you can also use cream of wheat.

Serves 4–6
Prep time: 10 minutes +
15 minutes standing
Cook time: 20 minutes

For the dhokla

170g/6oz/1 cup coarse
  semolina (sooji)

215g/7½oz/1 cup plain
  full-fat yogurt

125–160ml/4–5¼fl oz/
  ½–⅔ cup water

2 tsp Green Chilli Paste (page 32)

1 tsp Ginger Paste (page 32)

½ tsp sugar

salt, to taste

2 tsp oil, plus extra for greasing

1 tsp bicarbonate of soda
  (baking soda)

For the seasoning

3 tbsp oil

1 tbsp mustard seeds

2 green chillies, stems removed
  and thinly sliced

1 tbsp sesame seeds

To garnish

1 tbsp sweetened coconut flakes
  or grated fresh coconut

3 tbsp chopped coriander
  (cilantro)

To make the dhokla, combine all the ingredients, except the oil and bicarbonate of soda, in a bowl. Mix well, then set aside for 15 minutes. Stir in the oil.

Bring a medium steamer pan of water to the boil.

Place a heatproof or stainless-steel 23cm (9-inch) plate into the steamer (we traditionally use a thali here). Add the bicarbonate of soda to the batter and mix well. Pour the mixture into the heated plate, cover, and steam for 15 minutes over a medium heat. The dhokla is done when a cake tester (or fork) inserted in the centre comes out clean. If needed, steam for another 2–3 minutes.

Remove the dhokla from the steamer and set aside to cool. Cut into 4cm (1½-inch) squares.

For the seasoning, heat the oil in a frying pan or skillet over a medium-low heat. Add the mustard seeds and fry until they begin to crackle. Add the green chillies and sesame seeds and fry for 6–8 seconds. Add the seasoning on top of the dhokla.

Garnish with the coconut flakes and coriander, and serve with green garlic chutney (page 41), if you like.

CORN DELIGHT

MAKAI NO CHEVDO

GF Q

This tasty snack is common in Gujarat as it's quick to prepare once you have all the ingredients at hand. It is certainly a family favourite. Not only does my son think it's 'mind-blowing', but my father likened it to 'magic'. It's sweet (thanks to the natural sugars in the corn) and tangy (thanks to the acidity in the yogurt) and has just the right amount of punch from the addition of chilli. Of course, you can add more chilli to the recipe if you prefer it spicier, but I like it just as it's written here.

Serves 4
Prep time: 5 minutes
Cook time: 20–25 minutes

2 green chillies, stems removed

2 garlic cloves

900g/2lb sweetcorn (corn), thawed
   if frozen

3 tbsp oil

2 tsp mustard seeds

1 tsp cumin seeds

½ tsp asafoetida

1 tbsp Coriander-cumin Powder
   (page 29)

110g/3¾oz/½ cup plain
   full-fat yogurt

1½ tsp salt

3 tbsp chopped coriander
   (cilantro), to garnish

Place the chillies and garlic in a blender or food processor and blitz to achieve a coarse paste consistency. Add the corn and blitz for 20–30 seconds, stopping to scrape down the sides of the jug/bowl halfway through to ensure an even consistency. Set aside.

Heat the oil in a large frying pan or skillet over a medium heat. Add the mustard seeds and once they begin to crackle, add the cumin seeds and asafoetida. Add the corn mixture and coriander-cumin powder and reduce the heat to medium-low. Cover the pan partially with a lid and cook for 12–15 minutes, stirring occasionally. Stir in the yogurt and salt and cook for another 4–6 minutes.

Transfer to a serving dish, garnish with the coriander and serve warm.

GREEN GODDESS CHUTNEY PIZZA

This dish was inspired by a dining experience we had in Vancouver, Canada, where we were served complimentary naan with chutney on top. It reminded me of a cheese-less pizza. On our return home, I thought I would recreate it with mozzarella. After planning to make it in the oven, my daughter suggested I cook it on the hob (stovetop) – and it turned out fabulous!

There is an equally special story behind the pizza dough. On our third visit to Italy, I met a lady at the airport in Rome who shared my passion for good food. We got talking. It turned out she had recently taken a cooking lesson in Positano on the Amalfi coast and had 'the best' pizza dough recipe. Before my plane even took off, that lovely lady had emailed me the recipe. I was so touched by her enthusiasm and forever grateful to her for keeping her word and sending it to me. The love of food and cooking certainly has a way of bringing kind strangers into your life.

Serves 2
Prep time: 25–30 minutes +
2 hours proving
Cook time: 10–15 minutes

For the pizza

2 tsp easy-blend dried yeast (active dry yeast)

150ml/5fl oz/½ cup plus 3 tbsp lukewarm water

250g/8¾oz/1¼ cups plain (all-purpose) flour, plus extra for dusting

pinch of salt

cooking spray

140g/5oz/½ cup Green Garlic Chutney (page 41)

115–175g/4–6oz/1–1½ cups grated firm mozzarella cheese

Activate the yeast in 60ml/2fl oz/¼ cup of the lukewarm water in a small bowl. Set aside for several minutes. Sift the flour into a large bowl and add the salt. Create a well in the centre and pour in the yeast mixture. Use clean hands to combine the two, adding the remaining 90ml/3fl oz/ ¼ cup plus 3 tablespoons lukewarm water, and form into a dough. Dust a clean work surface with flour. Knead the dough for 10–15 minutes until it becomes elastic. Place the dough in a bowl. Cover with a clean, damp tea (dish) towel and allow to prove for 2 hours in a warm environment (approximately 22°C/72°F), until doubled in size.

Transfer the dough to a clean, lightly floured work surface. Divide the dough into two portions and use a rolling pin to roll each into a round about 3mm (⅛ inch) thick. Heat a large flat pan over a low heat and grease with cooking spray. Place one of the pizza bases onto the pan and cook for 2–3 minutes, until golden brown underneath. Carefully flip the pizza over, then spread half the chutney on top. Sprinkle half the mozzarella over it and cook for another 3–5 minutes until the cheese has melted. Transfer to a plate and repeat with the remaining pizza.

Serve immediately.

OKRA FRIES

BHINDA NA BHAJIYA

DF   VG

Deep-frying okra in a fantastically flavoured batter is a wonderful way to use this vegetable creatively. About ten years ago, we had very affluent guests from Surat visit us in the States. Surat is known as a foodie paradise, with exquisite delicacies and the most delicious street food, so I was somewhat intimidated by the prospect and nervous about what to serve them. I wanted the meal to be special, traditional and unique. After much anxiety I made these okra fries – and to my delight, they loved them. Surprisingly, they had never come across such an appetizer before, but to this day, they still talk about it when they call us. I couldn't ask for a better compliment from locals in the know. I love to serve these appetizers with masala chai and mint chutney.

Serves 4
Prep time: 10 minutes +
15 minutes standing
Cook time: 20 minutes

14 okras, wiped with a damp cloth or paper towel

700–950ml/24–32fl oz/3–4 cups oil, for deep-frying

Masala Chai (page 188) and Mint Chutney (page 42), to serve

For the batter
95g/3¼oz/¾ cup gram flour (besan)

30g/1oz/¼ cup rice flour

2 tbsp sesame seeds

1 tsp coriander seeds

1 tsp fennel seeds

1 tsp chilli powder

½ tsp ground turmeric

½ tsp garam masala

¼ tsp ajwain (carom) seeds

1 tsp black peppercorns

1 tsp Green Chilli Paste (page 32)

125ml/4fl oz/½ cup water

For the batter, combine all the ingredients in a bowl and whisk until smooth. Cover the mixture with a lid and set aside for 15 minutes.

Meanwhile, trim the ends of the okra and slice each in half lengthways. Cut the halves into matchstick-thin strips.

Heat the oil in a large deep saucepan, over a medium heat. Dip an okra strip, one at a time, into the batter until evenly coated. Remove and allow excess batter to drip off. Carefully lower 6 okra strips into the hot oil and fry for 1½–2 minutes until golden and crispy, moving them around in the oil using a metal slotted spoon or skimmer to prevent them from sticking together. Remove and drain on a tray lined with paper towels. Repeat this process until all the okras are fried.

Serve immediately with masala chai and mint chutney.

CHICKPEA PATTIES
CHANA TIKKI

GF   DF   VG

About two years ago, my husband and I decided to start following a healthier lifestyle. We discovered all the benefits of black gram (urad beans) and included it in our diet, particularly at breakfast time. Hearty, filling and quick to prepare, we love this with our morning tea. The batch can be made in advance and kept covered in the fridge for up to 4 days, making it the perfect grab-and-go breakfast, requiring only 3–5 minutes' cooking time.

The idea of having patties with green garlic chutney was not something I was familiar with, but I was inspired by a social media post I stumbled upon. Like most things in life, you never know how something will turn out until you try, and I am so glad I tried the combination. This is my version, which I have perfected over time. You should be able to find black gram, also known as kala chana, in an Indian grocery store.

Serves 4
Prep time: 10 minutes +
6 hours soaking
Cook time: 10–15 minutes

170g/6oz/1 cup dried black gram (kala chana)

750ml/26fl oz/3¼ cups cold water

1½ tsp Coriander-cumin Powder (page 29)

10g/⅓oz/¼ cup chopped coriander (cilantro)

2 garlic cloves

2 small green chillies, stems removed

2 tbsp gram flour (besan)

salt, to taste

1 small red onion, roughly chopped

oil, for frying

3 tbsp sesame seeds

Green Garlic Chutney (page 41) or Mint Chutney (page 42), to serve

Rinse the black gram and place in a bowl. Cover with 700ml/24fl oz/ 3 cups of the cold water and leave to soak for 6 hours or overnight.

Drain the black gram, then transfer them to a blender or food processor. Add the coriander-cumin powder, chopped coriander, garlic, chillies, gram flour and salt. Blitz for 3–5 minutes, stopping to scrape down the sides of the jug/bowl halfway to achieve a coarse consistency. Add the remaining 50ml/2fl oz/¼ cup water. Add the red onion and blitz for 6–8 seconds. Add a little more water if needed. Transfer the mixture to a bowl.

Heat a non-stick frying pan or skillet over a medium-low heat for 3–4 minutes. Add 1 teaspoon of oil and drop 2–3 tablespoons of the mixture into the pan, using the side of the spoon to shape into patties once in the pan. Scatter over the sesame seeds and cook for 2–2½ minutes on each side until golden brown. Cook the patties in two to three batches, using a teaspoon of oil before cooking the next batch.

Serve with green garlic or mint chutney.

CHICKPEA CRUMBLE CAKE

SURTI SEV KHAMANI

GF   DF   VG

Serves 4–6
Prep time: 15 minutes +
2 hours soaking
Cook time: 25 minutes

Just because we don't live in Surat, doesn't mean we can't enjoy the city's authentic dishes when the craving hits (as it often does with me). This dish is packed with all the flavours of Gujarat, and it makes for a healthy, gluten-free breakfast or snack. I like to serve it as an appetizer (along with chutney and thin sev).

For the dal

180g/6¼oz/1 cup dried split chickpeas (chana dal)

350ml/12fl oz/1½ cups water

7.5cm (3-inch) piece of fresh ginger, peeled and chopped

3 green chillies, stems removed

3 garlic cloves

¼ tsp bicarbonate of soda (baking soda)

salt, to taste

For the seasoning

4 tbsp oil

1½ tsp mustard seeds

¼ tsp asafoetida

5 dried red chillies

2 tbsp sugar

¾ tsp ground turmeric

To serve

45–60g/1½–2oz/¾–1 cup nylon thin sev (crunchy noodles)

15g/½oz/⅓ cup chopped coriander (cilantro)

115g/4oz/¾ cup pomegranate seeds

Green Garlic Chutney (page 41)

1½ limes, cut into wedges

Put the split chickpeas and the water in a bowl and soak for 2 hours.

Place the ginger, chillies and garlic in a blender or food processor and blitz for 40–50 seconds. Add the soaked split chickpeas and soaking water to the blender, along with the bicarbonate of soda, salt and 6 tablespoons of fresh water. Blitz for 10–15 seconds, stopping to scrape down the sides of the jug/bowl halfway to achieve a coarse consistency. Set aside.

Place a heatproof or stainless-steel 28cm (11-inch) plate into a steamer (we traditionally use a thali) and pour the mixture into it. Cover and steam for 15–18 minutes. Remove the plate from the steamer and allow the mixture to cool. Crumble it with your hands then set aside.

For the seasoning, heat the oil in a frying pan or skillet over a medium heat and add the mustard seeds. Once they begin to crackle, add the asafoetida and the dried chillies. Add the sugar and 125ml/4fl oz/½ cup water and cook for 1–2 minutes. Tip in the dal mixture and the turmeric and stir well to combine. Add another 185ml/6fl oz/¾ cup water and cover the pan, cooking over a low heat for 4–5 minutes and stirring occasionally. Add another 2–4 tablespoons of water if the mixture looks a little dry.

Transfer to a serving bowl. Garnish with the thin sev, chopped coriander and pomegranate seeds and serve warm with green garlic chutney and lime wedges.

SPICY PEA CROQUETTES

KACHORI

DF   VG

Makes 12
Prep time: 20 minutes + cooling
Cook time: 20–25 minutes

Every recipe tells a story, and this one is no exception. When I was pregnant with my youngest, my mother-in-law would make kachoris for breakfasts at the weekends. We feasted on them until we couldn't eat any more. Here, the coconut adds a lovely Surti element. A food processor speeds things up, if you have one.

For the filling

5cm (2-inch) piece of fresh ginger

3 green chillies, stems removed

450g/1lb/3½ cups shelled petits pois or peas, thawed if frozen

1 tbsp oil, plus 700–950ml/24–32fl oz/3–4 cups oil, for deep-frying

pinch of asafoetida

3 tbsp raisins

3 tbsp cashew nuts, roughly chopped

2 tbsp grated fresh coconut or sweetened coconut flakes

10g/⅓oz/¼ cup finely chopped coriander (cilantro)

¾ tsp garam masala

salt, to taste

2 tsp fresh lime juice

1½ tsp sugar

For the dough

200g/7oz/1½ cups plain (all-purpose) flour

3–4 tbsp oil

5 tbsp plus 2 tsp warm water

chutney, to serve

For the filling, peel the ginger and blitz with the chillies in a blender or food processor for 1 minute. Add the peas and blitz for 15–20 seconds to a coarse consistency.

Heat the tablespoon of oil in a non-stick frying pan or skillet over a medium heat. Add the asafoetida and cook for 5–7 seconds. Add the pea mixture and cook for 2–3 minutes, stirring occasionally. Reduce the heat to medium-low.

Add the raisins, cashews, coconut, coriander, garam masala and salt and cook for 10 minutes. Stir in the lime juice and sugar and mix well. Remove the pan from the heat. Allow to cool slightly so the mixture is easier to handle. Shape into 12 balls, approximately 4cm (1½ inches) in diameter and set aside.

For the dough, combine the flour and oil in a bowl. Mix well and add the warm water. Knead for 2–3 minutes until the dough is smooth and soft. Add a little more water if needed. Divide the dough into 12 equal portions. Roll each portion into a disc, about 10cm (4 inches) in diameter.

Take the filling portions and arrange one in the centre of each dough disc. Bring the sides of the dough together like a parcel and pinch the top to seal. Trim off any excess dough from the pinched end.

Heat the oil for deep-frying in a deep saucepan over a medium heat. To avoid overcrowding, carefully lower in half the kachori and deep-fry for 2–4 minutes, using a slotted spoon to move them around, until they are golden all over. Using a metal slotted spoon or skimmer, transfer to a tray lined with paper towels to drain. Repeat with the remaining kachori, then serve hot with your favourite chutney.

SPINACH DUMPLINGS
PALAK NA MUTHIYA

 GF

Serves 4
Prep time: 15 minutes
Cook time: 25–30 minutes

For the dumplings

125g/4½oz/1 cup gram flour
  (besan)

110g/3¾oz/½ cup plain full-fat
  yogurt

2 tbsp oil

1½ tbsp Green Chilli Paste
  (page 32)

1 tsp Ginger Paste (page 32)

1½ tsp fenugreek seeds

1½ tsp Coriander-cumin Powder
  (page 29)

1 tbsp sugar

½ tsp ground turmeric

¾ tsp salt, or to taste

225–280g/8–10oz baby or regular
  spinach leaves, washed and
  patted dry

For the seasoning

3 tbsp oil

2 tbsp chopped garlic

1 tbsp sesame seeds

2 tbsp sweetened coconut flakes,
  to garnish

Healthy, nutritious eating has never tasted this good! I like to think of these palak na muthiya as my signature dish.

The dumplings are low in calories and jam-packed with flavour. Thanks to the addition of baby spinach (a powerhouse of nutrients) and gram flour, they are fantastic for digestion and act as a slow-release fuel – great for avoiding blood-sugar spikes.

Hugely versatile as an appetizer or a main meal, it's a great option to take palak na muthiya along to an event – they can be made in under an hour ahead of time and stored in the fridge for 3–4 days. The dumplings can be served with oil or chutney, but I don't think you'll need either as this recipe includes a delicious garlic-and-sesame seasoning with sweet coconut flakes to serve. Amazing!

Bring 1–1.2 litres/34–40fl oz/4–5 cups water to the boil in a steamer. In a bowl, combine all the ingredients for the dumplings, except for the spinach, and mix well.

If using regular spinach leaves, chop them smaller. Stir the spinach into the bowl and mix well. Using your hand, keep mixing and kneading until the mixture is fully incorporated. Divide into three. Shape each third into an oval about 10cm (4 inches) long and 4cm (1½ inches) wide. Place in the steamer. Cover and steam for 18–20 minutes. The dumplings are done when a cake tester (or fork) inserted in the centre comes out clean. If not, steam for another 2 minutes. Remove the dumplings from the steamer and allow to cool. Once cool, slice into 1cm (½-inch) thick pieces.

To make the seasoning, heat the oil in a pan over a low-medium heat. Add the garlic and fry for 1–2 minutes until lightly caramelized. Add the sesame seeds and fry for just a few seconds. Add the sliced dumplings and cook, turning, for 3–4 minutes.

Transfer to a serving plate, garnish with the coconut flakes and serve.

PANEER TIKKA

GF

Serves 4
Prep time: 10 minutes +
4 hours chilling
Cook time: 5–10 minutes

110g/3¾oz/½ cup plain
  full-fat yogurt

1½ tsp Kashmiri chilli powder
  or regular chilli powder

1½ tsp garam masala

¼ tsp ground turmeric

1¼ tsp salt

1 tbsp oil

2½ tsp Garlic Paste (page 31)

1 tbsp plus 1 tsp fresh lemon juice

3–4 drops red food colouring
  (optional)

280g/10oz paneer, cut into 7.5 x
  2.5cm (3- x 1-inch) slices

3–4 tbsp butter

To serve
4 lemon wedges

½ red onion, finely sliced

Mint Chutney (page 42)

I was fortunate enough to be given cooking lessons from a Maldivian chef in 2013. Imagine my delight when I learnt he was Indian and was including Indian dishes in my lesson. His overall philosophy was to use the freshest ingredients possible. To add to the wonderful experience of learning so much from him, we got to enjoy the dishes together afterwards.

This particular dish is one I cherish from that lesson. After some research, I modified a simple version to suit my way of cooking and personal taste. Paneer is a fresh, crumbly cheese widely used in vegetarian dishes. I make paneer tikka all the time now, either as a snack or an appetizer, or to enhance the flavour of a paneer curry. It is equally suitable as a quick, tasty lunch for the kids.

In a bowl, combine the yogurt, chilli powder, garam masala, ground turmeric and salt and mix well. Add the oil, garlic paste, lemon juice and food colouring, if using. Add the paneer and, using clean hands or a spoon, gently and evenly coat the paneer in the marinade. Cover and refrigerate for 4 hours or overnight (the longer the better).

Melt the butter in a non-stick frying pan or skillet over a medium heat, swirling the pan to ensure the base is evenly coated. Place the marinated paneer in the pan and fry the pieces for 2–4 minutes on each side until golden brown.

Transfer to a serving platter and serve with lemon wedges and the red onion slices. Enjoy this with mint chutney.

Appetizers

KUTCHI DABELI

Serves 4–6
Prep time: 25 minutes
Cook time: 45–60 minutes

For the dabeli masala
5–7 fresh curry leaves

3–4 dried red chillies

3–4 cloves

¼ tsp broken cinnamon stick

1 black cardamom pod

1 bay leaf

2 tbsp coriander seeds

1 tsp mango powder (amchur)

½ tsp fennel seeds

½ tsp salt

¼ tsp cumin seeds

2 tbsp desiccated (dried shredded)
   coconut

1½ tsp sesame seeds

For the red garlic chutney
6 garlic cloves

3 tbsp Kashmiri chilli powder

½ tsp sesame seeds

½ tsp salt

60ml/2fl oz/¼ cup water

For the spiced peanuts
1 tbsp oil

45g/1½oz/⅓ cup raw or
   roasted peanuts

1 tsp chilli powder

Kutchi dabeli is a tasty Indian spicy potato burger that originated in Mandvi, a city in Kutch, and we Gujarati enjoy it as much as Americans love their burgers. In fact, it can be found all across India! While the tamarind and green chutneys, dabeli masala and spiced peanuts can be bought from Indian supermarkets, the homemade versions are infinitely better.

Heat a frying pan or skillet over a low heat. Add all the ingredients for the dabeli masala, except the desiccated coconut and sesame seeds, and roast, stirring occasionally, for 3–4 minutes, until slightly brown and fragrant. Add the coconut and sesame seeds and roast for another minute. Set aside to cool.

Transfer the cooled mixture to a blender and grind to a coarse powder. This recipe requires only 2 tablespoons; store the rest in an airtight container for up to 6 months.

Put all the ingredients for the red garlic chutney in a blender, and blend to a smooth paste. Transfer the chutney to an airtight glass container. This recipe requires only 3 tablespoons; store the rest in the fridge for up to a week.

For the spiced peanuts, heat the oil in a frying pan or skillet over a medium heat. Add the peanuts and roast for 3–4 minutes, then add the chilli powder and a pinch of salt and mix well. Set aside to cool.

For the masala paste

2 tbsp Dabeli Masala
  (see opposite)

2 tbsp Sweet Tamarind Chutney
  (page 45)

60ml/2fl oz/¼ cup water

For the potato filling

4 potatoes, peeled

2 tbsp oil

½ tsp salt, plus extra to taste

2–3 tbsp finely chopped onion

2 tbsp nylon thin sev (crunchy
  noodles)

2 tbsp fresh pomegranate seeds

1 tbsp grated fresh coconut

1 tbsp finely chopped coriander
  (cilantro)

To assemble and finish

4–6 dinner rolls (pav)

3 tbsp Green Garlic Chutney
  (page 41)

3 tbsp Sweet Tamarind Chutney
  (page 45)

3 tbsp Red Garlic Chutney
  (see opposite)

60g/2oz/¼ cup butter

15g/½oz/¼ cup nylon thin sev
  (crunchy noodles)

Combine the ingredients for the masala paste, mix well and set aside.

To make the dabeli, put the potatoes in a saucepan with enough water to cover. Bring to the boil, then reduce to a medium-high heat and cook, partially covered, for 25–30 minutes, until cooked through. Drain, then allow to cool. Mash and set aside.

Heat the oil in a frying pan or skillet over a medium heat. Add the prepared masala paste and cook for 8–10 seconds, stirring continuously. Add the mashed potatoes and salt and cook for a further 2–4 minutes, mixing well.

Transfer the potato mixture to a plate and top with the onion, sev, pomegranate seeds, coconut, coriander and the spiced peanuts.

To assemble the dish, cut the dinner rolls in half, leaving a hinge on one edge. Spread 2 teaspoons of all three chutneys on the base of each roll. Stuff the potato dabeli mixture into the rolls.

Melt the butter in a frying pan or skillet over a medium heat, until sizzling. Add the rolls to the pan and fry the bottoms for 2–3 minutes, until toasted and slightly golden. Carefully flip and fry the other side for another 2 minutes.

Place the sev on a shallow plate. Dab the sides with the exposed filling into the sev and serve immediately.

BAKED SPICY CAKES
HANDVO

GF

Serves 8
Prep time: 15–20 minutes +
3–4 hours soaking +
12–14 hours fermenting
Cook time: 30 minutes

For the handvo

185g/6½oz/1 cup white or
  brown rice

90g/3¼oz/½ cup dried split pigeon
  peas (toor dal)

2–3 tbsp Green Chilli Paste
  (page 32)

1 tbsp Pickle Masala (page 34)

1 tbsp plus 1 tsp grated jaggery
  (gur) or brown sugar

1½ tbsp Ginger Paste (page 32)

2 tsp Coriander-cumin Powder
  (page 29)

½ tsp ground turmeric

½ tsp ajwain (carom) seeds

¼ tsp asafoetida

2 tsp salt, or to taste

110g/3¾oz/½ cup plain
  full-fat yogurt

2 tbsp oil, plus extra for greasing

130g/4½oz/1½ cups grated
  courgette (zucchini), bottle
  gourd (doodhi), or shredded
  cabbage

40g/1½oz/⅓ cup shelled petits pois
  or peas, thawed if frozen

45g/1½oz/⅓ cup sweetcorn (corn),
  thawed if frozen

In ancient times, this mixture would be put in a covered broad-based vessel and cooked on a wooden or coal fire with glowing red-hot coals placed on the lid for it to bake and develop a lovely brown crust. The mouth-watering aroma would waft around the neighbourhood and everyone would know who was going to have a great dinner that evening! No such luck with electric ovens…

While I have made significant changes to this recipe over the years, I must give credit to a friend who shared her recipe with me more than twenty-five years ago. Initially, I'll admit I wasn't a fan of it, but I came to love it. It's packed with vegetables, making it high in fibre and very nutritious – not what you might expect from a dish described as 'cake'! And if you prefer brown rice to white, even better! My foodie husband is particularly fond of handvo, and thankfully it stores well, covered in the fridge for up to five days.

Rinse the rice and split pigeon peas, then soak them in 700ml/24fl oz/ 3 cups water for 3–4 hours.

Drain, then transfer the rice and pigeon peas to a food processor and blitz for 40 seconds to a coarse texture. Add another 60ml/2fl oz/¼ cup water if needed and blitz again for 35–40 seconds, still retaining a coarse consistency. Transfer the batter to a bowl, cover and leave to ferment overnight or for at least 12–14 hours, depending on weather conditions and ambient temperature. The batter should rise by about 20–30 per cent.

Preheat the oven to 200°C fan/220°C/425°F/gas mark 7. Grease a 12-hole muffin pan or a 20cm (8 inch) round cake tin (baking pan) with oil.

To the bowl of fermented batter add the remaining ingredients except for the courgettes, peas and corn. Mix well, then stir in the courgettes, peas and corn and mix well again.

Pour 60ml/2fl oz/¼ cup batter into each cup of the muffin pan, or pour all the batter into the prepared cake tin, spreading it out evenly.

For the seasoning

3–4 tbsp oil

2 tbsp mustard seeds

5–6 dried red chillies

½ tsp asafoetida

2 tbsp sesame seeds

To make the seasoning, heat the oil in a frying pan or skillet over a medium heat. Add the mustard seeds and, once the seeds begin to crackle, add the chillies, asafoetida and sesame seeds and remove the pan from the heat. Sprinkle 1–2 teaspoons of the seasoning on top of each muffin. If making one cake, sprinkle the seasoning over the surface of the handvo.

Bake on the middle rack for 26–28 minutes. (If using a cake tin, bake for 25–30 minutes.) The handvo is cooked when a cake tester (or fork) inserted in the centre comes out clean. If not, continue to bake for another 3–4 minutes. Serve hot or at room temperature.

Optional: Brown the top by switching the oven to the grill (broiler) setting. Grill for 2 minutes until the top turns a light golden brown. Keep your eye on it, as it doesn't take long to colour. Allow to cool for 10 minutes before removing from the pan.

SPICY POTATO CROQUETTES

KAJU DRAKSH BATATA VADA

GF   DF   VG

Serves 4–5
Prep time: 20 minutes
Cook time: 15–20 minutes

For the paste
3 green chillies, stems removed

2 garlic cloves

2.5cm (1-inch) piece of fresh
   ginger, peeled

For the croquettes
4 potatoes, unpeeled

1 tbsp oil

½ tsp ground turmeric

¾ tsp garam masala

salt, to taste

3 tbsp chopped raw cashew nuts

12 raisins

10g/⅓oz/¼ cup chopped
   coriander (cilantro)

25g/1oz/¼ cup chopped garlic
   scapes (optional)

1½ tsp sugar

1 tsp lime juice

For the batter
150g/5½oz/1¼ cups gram flour
   (besan)

2 tbsp rice flour

¼ tsp ground turmeric

¾ tsp salt

3 tbsp sesame seeds, lightly crushed

Batata vada is a popular Gujarati appetizer throughout India. The best part of this lip-smacking dish is that you eat it piping hot as soon as it comes out of the fryer. You'll see many an Indian street-food stall with people gathered around eagerly awaiting a small plate of vada with a healthy serving of tamarind or green chutney. When my mom used to make these, she would fry five or six at a time and offer one to each of us, to avoid a fight. We would chat while waiting for the second and third, and fourth, offering. I try to follow that way of serving today, and it works brilliantly for my family as well as guests.

To make the paste, combine all the ingredients in a blender and blend until a smooth paste is formed. Set aside.

For the croquettes, put the potatoes in a medium-sized microwave-safe bowl and add 480ml/16fl oz/2 cups water. Cover the bowl and heat on high for 8–10 minutes. Carefully remove the potatoes, drain and allow to cool. When cool enough to handle, peel and mash. Set aside.

Heat the oil in a pan over a medium heat. Add the ground turmeric and garam masala and cook for 4–6 seconds. Add the potatoes, the paste and salt to taste. Stir as it cooks for 3–4 minutes. Mix in the cashew nuts, raisins, coriander and garlic scapes, if using. Remove the pan from the heat, stir in the sugar and lime juice, and set aside to cool. Once the mixture is cool enough to handle, divide into 12–15 equal-sized portions and shape each one into a ball. Set aside.

For the batter, combine all the ingredients with 135ml/4½fl oz/½ cup plus 2 tbsp warm water and whisk until smooth.

Heat 700–950ml/24–32fl oz/3–4 cups oil, for deep-frying, in a deep saucepan over a medium heat. Working in batches to avoid overcrowding, dip a few potato croquettes at a time into the batter and carefully lower into the hot oil using a metal slotted spoon. Deep-fry for 30–40 seconds, until golden brown all over. Remove with a slotted spoon or skimmer and place onto a tray lined with paper towels to drain the excess oil. Repeat the process until all the croquettes are deep-fried and serve hot, with mint chutney (page 42), if you like.

FLATTENED RICE WITH NUT AND SPICE

BATATA PAUVA

GF DF VG Q

Serves 3–4
Prep time: 5–10 minutes
Cook time: 15–20 minutes

165g/5¾oz/1½ cups thick flattened rice flakes (thick pauva/poha)

60ml/2fl oz/¼ cup water

2 tbsp oil

1 tsp mustard seeds

1 tsp cumin seeds

pinch of asafoetida

1 potato, peeled and cut into 1cm (½-inch) cubes

½ tsp ground turmeric

2–3 tbsp raw or roasted cashew nuts

8–10 sultanas (golden raisins)

2 small green chillies, stems removed and thinly sliced

salt, to taste

2 tsp fresh lime juice

2 tsp sugar

2 tbsp chopped coriander (cilantro)

1 lemon, cut into wedges, to serve

Flattened rice, pauva or poha, is a type of Indian rice flake that is generally parboiled before flattening so that it can cook quickly. I've eaten many variations of this popular breakfast dish across India, but none of them compares to the Gujarati version. The flattened rice is the perfect foil for the fragrant spices, chillies and potato (in other parts of India, it is prepared with onion).

Place the flattened rice in a colander and rinse. Sprinkle the water over the flattened rice, then set aside over a plate while preparing the potatoes. (The flattened rice should absorb all the water.)

Heat the oil in a frying pan or skillet over a medium heat. Add the mustard seeds and fry until they begin to crackle. Add the cumin seeds and asafoetida. Stir in the potato and ground turmeric, turn down the heat to medium-low and sauté for 8–10 minutes, until cooked through.

Add the cashew nuts, sultanas, chillies and salt. Stir continuously for 3–4 minutes. Add the drained flattened rice, lime juice, sugar and coriander and gently stir to avoid breaking up the flattened rice. Cook for another 2 minutes to bring together. The pauva will look like loose rice.

Serve hot with lemon wedges.

LAYERED TARO LEAVES
PATRA

GF

Taro (patra) leaves are an excellent source of fibre, antioxidants and polyphenols, which offer numerous health benefits. Here, nutrient-dense taro, gram flour (besan), yogurt and spices combine to provide a healthy and tasty snack for meat-free Mondays. Make sure you look for taro leaves with black stems, as those with green stems can cause a stinging sensation in the mouth. Spring (collard) greens can be a great option if you are unable to find taro leaves – the result is just as good!

Serves 4
Prep time: 25 minutes
Cook time: 20–25 minutes

12 taro (patra) leaves, or 1 bunch spring (collard) greens, washed and dried

For the besan paste
185g/6½oz/1½ cups gram flour (besan)

2 tsp Ginger Paste (page 32)

2 tbsp Green Chilli Paste (page 32)

2 tsp fenugreek seeds

½ tsp ground turmeric

¾ tsp garam masala

1 tbsp white or brown sugar

110g/3¾oz/½ cup plain full-fat yogurt

¾ tsp salt, or to taste

1½ tbsp oil

2 tbsp water

For the seasoning
2½ tbsp oil

1½ tsp mustard seeds

1 tbsp sesame seeds

2 tbsp sweetened coconut flakes, to garnish

To make the besan paste, combine all the ingredients in a medium bowl and mix until smooth.

Using a knife, carefully trim off the stem and veins from the taro leaves or spring greens, keeping the dark green side of the leaf facing downwards. Lay a leaf on a chopping board, with the tip of the leaf facing towards you, then use your fingertips to spread out a thin layer of paste on top.

Place another leaf on top and repeat the process so that you have 3–4 layers in total. (The size of the leaves will vary. You can make 3–4 layers, depending on the desired thickness of the roll.) Fold the sides inwards by about 2.5cm (1 inch), then roll up tightly and set aside. Make 2–3 more rolls.

Set up a steamer and steam the rolls for 18–20 minutes over a medium heat. The taro leaf is cooked when a cake tester (or fork) inserted in the centre comes out clean. Slice into 1cm (½-inch) thick pieces.

For the seasoning, heat the oil in a large frying pan or skillet over a medium heat and add the mustard seeds. Once they begin to crackle, add the sesame seeds and taro rolls. Reduce the heat to low and gently stir for 2 minutes, to prevent the rolls from breaking.

Transfer to a plate and garnish with coconut flakes. Serve with masala chai (page 188).

CRISPY TARO POTLI

PATRA POTLI

DF · Q

A little patience and practice may be required to make these, but the results will be worth all your effort. Not only are they filled with layered taro leaves (patra), rather than the potatoes and peas of a traditional samosa (see page 102), but they are simply beautiful to look at. I first tried these at my cousin's wedding and whenever I taste them, I am transported back to my favourite childhood farsan place.

The layered taro leaves can be homemade (see opposite), but it does require a degree of time, so you can use frozen patra, which are available in Indian supermarkets.

I encourage you to prepare the potli with this layered taro leaves filling, but they would be equally delightful with a traditional potato-and-pea samosa filling. These little perfect pouches (potlis) of deliciousness are such a hit at my small dinner parties, and they can be at yours too…

Serves 4–5
Prep time: 20 minutes
Cook time: 6 minutes

3–4 spring onions (scallions)

240ml/8fl oz/1 cup water

2 rolls Layered Taro Leaves (opposite), or you can use store-bought frozen patra, thawed

8 spring roll wrappers

700–950ml/24–32fl oz/3–4 cups oil, for deep-frying

Green Garlic Chutney (page 41), to serve

Remove the white ends of the spring onions and set aside for another use. (You need only the green parts in this recipe, to tie the pouches.) Bring the water to the boil in a small saucepan and blanch the green parts of the spring onions for 2–4 seconds, then immediately remove and pat dry on paper towels. Set aside.

To make the potlis, spoon 2½–3 tablespoons of the layered taro leaves onto the centre of each spring roll wrapper. Lift the edges of the wrappers and bring them together, scrunching to form a sealed bundle around the filling. Use the green parts of the spring onion to tie and secure the pouches closed.

Heat the oil in a deep saucepan and, once hot, carefully lower the potlis into the oil, cooking over a medium heat for 2–3 minutes until they are golden brown all over. If necessary, work in batches to avoid overcrowding. Remove with a metal slotted spoon or skimmer and place on a tray lined with paper towels.

Serve hot with green garlic chutney.

CRISPY SAMOSAS

Serves 5
Prep time: 20 minutes +
20 minutes cooling
Cook time: 15–25 minutes

Making samosas takes a bit of patience and practice, but the results are worth it. Thankfully, good-quality ready-made puff pastry is available in all stores, so you can focus on the delicious filling and the careful preparation. Crispy and packed with flavour, these are fantastic served with Mint Chutney.

3 potatoes, unpeeled

480ml/16fl oz/2 cups water

1 tbsp oil, plus 700–950ml/
  24–32fl oz/3–4 cups for
  deep-frying and greasing

½ tsp cumin seeds

¼ tsp ground turmeric

½ tsp garam masala

40g/1½oz/⅓ cup shelled petits pois
  or peas, thawed if frozen

2 tbsp Green Chilli Paste
  (page 32)

20g/¾oz/½ cup chopped
  coriander (cilantro)

25g/1oz/¼ cup chopped garlic
  scapes or ½ tsp Garlic Paste
  (page 31)

salt, to taste

1 tsp fresh lime juice

2 tsp sugar

245g/8¾oz store-bought puff
  pastry, thawed if frozen

Mint Chutney (page 42), to serve

Put the potatoes in a medium-sized microwave-safe bowl with the water. Cover the bowl and microwave for 8–10 minutes. Drain and leave to cool for 20 minutes. When the potatoes are cool enough to handle, peel and roughly chop. Set aside.

Heat the tablespoon of oil in a pan over a medium heat and add the cumin seeds. Once the seeds crackle, add the ground turmeric and garam masala. Cook for 10 seconds. Add the peas and cook for 3–5 minutes until the peas are tender. Add the potatoes, green chilli paste, coriander, garlic and salt and stir to mix well. Cook for 4–5 minutes, then remove the pan from the heat and add the lime juice and sugar. Mix well. Set aside to cool.

Trim the puff pastry sheets into ten 6cm (2½-inch) squares. Roll a square into a cone, sealing the edge with water. Fill the cone with 1½ tablespoons of the filling and fold in the longer end of the cone, giving the cone structure to stay upright when placed on a flat surface. Use a little more water to seal the edges of the cone, fully enclosing the filling. Repeat the process until all the samosas are made.

Heat the oil for deep-frying in a deep saucepan over a medium heat. Working in batches to avoid overcrowding, carefully lower the samosas into the oil with a metal slotted spoon and reduce the heat to medium-low. Use the spoon to move them around and deep-fry for 2–3 minutes, until golden brown.

Remove the samosas with the spoon and drain on a tray lined with paper towels. Serve hot with mint chutney.

YELLOW PANCAKES

PANKI

GF

This authentic dish is unlike any pancake you will have ever had! A batter is created using rice and yogurt and seasoned with beautiful fragrant spices. It is then wrapped in a banana leaf and cooked to perfection.

It's a fun way of eating with your friends and family, as the banana leaves (which are not harmful but shouldn't be consumed) are peeled away, revealing the beautiful, bright-yellow pancakes, which can then be enjoyed with chutney. Fresh and frozen banana leaves are available at most Asian stores. If frozen, thaw thoroughly and pat dry before using.

Serves 4
Prep time: 10 minutes +
30 minutes standing
Cook time: 15–25 minutes

125g/4½oz/1 cup rice flour

290ml/10fl oz/1¼ cups water

2 tbsp plain full-fat yogurt

3–4 tsp Green Chilli Paste
(page 32)

¾ tsp Garlic Paste (page 31)

1 tsp Ginger Paste (page 32)

10g/⅓oz/¼ cup finely chopped
coriander (cilantro)

¾ tsp Coriander-cumin Powder
(page 29)

¾ tsp salt, or to taste

½ tsp ground turmeric

1 tbsp oil

2 banana leaves

cooking spray, for greasing

Green Garlic Chutney (page 41),
to serve

In a bowl, combine the rice flour, water and yogurt with the chilli, garlic and ginger pastes, then stir in the coriander, coriander-cumin powder, salt, turmeric and oil and mix well. Set aside for 30 minutes.

Wash the banana leaves and pat dry with paper towel. Trim the leaves into 8–10 discs, 13cm (5 inches) in diameter. You need to have an even number of discs, as they will be paired up. Spray one side of each disc with a little cooking spray.

To cook the panki, spray a flat griddle (grill pan), large frying pan or skillet with cooking spray and heat over a medium heat for 2–3 minutes. Place one disc of banana leaf in the pan, greased side facing up. Pour 3 tablespoons of the batter onto the banana leaf and spread it to make a thin layer, covering the leaf. Take a second banana leaf and place on top of the batter, greased side down, gently pressing down. Cook the panki for 2 minutes, then gently flip and cook for another 1–2 minutes, until blisters are visible on the banana leaves. Transfer to a plate and set aside. Repeat the process until all the panki are cooked, spraying with cooking spray before cooking each one. (Any leftover batter can be covered and stored in the fridge for up to 2 days.)

Serve hot and allow your guests to peel away the banana leaves and enjoy the panki with chutney.

Appetizers

THALI

Ah the thali! This is the special jewel in the crown that Gujarat has bestowed on Indian cuisine. The thali is a complete meal (the term means 'full meal on a plate'), both in terms of nutritional balance as well as taste! And what a visual feast: a large metal plate with small colourful bowls (vadkis) filled with at least three different vegetables, one kathol (pulses/legumes), a dal or kadhi, a curd-based raita and, filling the rest of the plate, a kachumber (salad), a couple of pickles and some chutney, papadums, flatbreads (roti/rotli, bhakhri or rotlo) and rice/khichdi. The sweet dish is placed beside the plate, together with a glass of thin buttermilk (chaas). As you sit down to begin the meal, the roti are served hot and all items replenished as you want them.

As a restaurant product the thali first made an appearance sometime back in the seventies. It was so popular that it spawned several other thalis – the Punjabi thali, Rajasthani thali, Bengali thali, and so on. What continues to bemuse me, however, is why Gujarati families, who generally have DBRS (Dal-Bhaat-Rotli-Shaak) for lunch almost every day, would want to go out to a restaurant and dine on the same thing? But that's Gujaratis for you!

DALS & SOUPS

A TRADITIONAL GUJARATI LUNCH

In most traditional Gujarati homes, the
lunch menu consists of dal and rice (called
dal-bhaat) or Yellow Rice (page 184) and
Spiced Yogurt Soup (page 125) (also known
as khichdi-kadhi). It is served with other
items such as roti, some form of vegetable
dish (shaak), and Kachumber (page 49).
These highly nutritious meals are a staple
in Gujarati households.

As the adage goes, variety is the spice
of life and dal is no exception. We like to
use a variety of dals – from black gram to
butter (lima) beans to mung beans – because
they provide the much-needed protein and
nourishment.

While these dishes are served in other parts
of India, what separates a Gujarati dal from all
other regions is the unique addition of jaggery
(which can be substituted with brown or white
sugar). Gujarati dal and kadhi are utterly
original and make a lasting impression.

CREAMY MASOOR DAL

GF

Serves 4
Prep time: 15 minutes +
2 hours soaking
Cook time: 1¼–1½ hours

130g/4½oz/¾ cup whole dried
  lentils (masoor) – brown are
  a good option

1.4 litres/48fl oz/6 cups water

3 tomatoes, roughly chopped

1 tsp Garlic Paste (page 31)

1 tsp salt, plus extra to taste

2 tbsp oil

¾ tsp cumin seeds

60g/2oz/½ cup chopped onion

1 tsp Ginger Paste (page 32)

1½ tsp Green Chilli Paste
  (page 32)

¼ tsp ground turmeric

1 tsp Coriander-cumin Powder
  (page 29)

½ tsp garam masala

½ tsp chilli powder

4–5 tbsp double (heavy) cream

10g/⅓oz/¼ cup chopped coriander
  (cilantro)

rice or Pooris (page 167), to serve

The idea for this recipe originally came from a Punjabi friend, but I've adapted it over the years. Firstly, the addition of homemade garlic paste turns a good recipe into a great recipe. The second alteration was a result of my son Aamir's intervention one night, turning a great recipe into a genius one! Trying to steer clear of the greasy, restaurant-style rich dal (which is made with plenty of butter), my son suggested we omit the butter and instead stir through some cream at the end and cook it a little longer: perfection!

Rinse the lentils, place them in a deep saucepan and cover with the water. Leave to soak for 2 hours. Bring the lentils and soaking water to the boil, then partially cover with a lid and cook over a medium heat for 30 minutes. Add the chopped tomatoes, garlic paste and salt, cover and cook for another 20–25 minutes until the lentils are tender.

At the same time, heat the oil in a separate pan over a medium heat and add the cumin seeds. Once they begin to crackle, add the onion and cook for 10 minutes over a low heat. Add the ginger paste, green chilli paste, ground turmeric, coriander-cumin powder, garam masala, chilli powder and salt to taste. Mix well and cook for another 3–4 minutes, stirring regularly. Pour the onion seasoning into the pan of lentils and cook for 10–12 minutes. Add 125ml/4fl oz/½ cup water, if needed, to achieve a thick soup consistency. Stir in the cream and coriander. Cook for another 3–5 minutes, then serve.

Transfer to a serving bowl and serve with rice or pooris.

Dals & Soups

RED LENTIL DAL

LAL MASOOR DAL

GF DF VG

It was my darling grandmother who insisted dal benefits from an hour of soaking before cooking, and how correct she was. I follow her instructions to this day. This dal recipe is one I am particularly proud of. Apart from the soaking time, it really doesn't take long to prepare, and the ingredients are uncomplicated. One day (in one of my many kitchen experiments), I made a dal using curry leaves and tomatoes and realized how perfectly these two simple ingredients complement each other! The result was a light and colourful dish that I now make very often.

Serves 2
Prep time: 10 minutes +
1 hour soaking
Cook time: 35–40 minutes

130g/4½oz/¾ cup dry split red lentils (lal masoor dal)

700ml/24fl oz/3 cups water

1 tsp Coriander-cumin Powder (page 29)

2 small ripe tomatoes, chopped into 2.5cm (1-inch) pieces

1 green chilli, stem removed and slit in half

½ tsp ground turmeric

salt, to taste

1½ tbsp oil

¼ tsp cumin seeds

1½ tbsp chopped garlic

3–5 dried red chillies

8–10 fresh curry leaves

¼ tsp Kashmiri chilli powder

2 tbsp chopped coriander (cilantro), to garnish

rice or chapatis, to serve

Wash the split red lentils under cold, running water three times and soak in a saucepan with the water for 1 hour. Over a medium-high heat cook the soaked lentils until tender, approximately 18–20 minutes. Add the coriander-cumin powder, tomatoes, green chilli, ground turmeric, salt and 350ml/12fl oz/1½ cups water to the dal and cook over a medium heat for 8–10 minutes.

Heat the oil in a deep saucepan and add the cumin seeds. Once the seeds begin to crackle, add the garlic. Cook over a medium heat until the garlic has turned a light brown colour. Add the dried chillies and curry leaves. Mix well and cook for 4–5 seconds. Add the chilli powder to the seasoning, then pour the seasoning over the dal. Mix well, stirring to combine and cook over a low heat for another 8–10 minutes, adding a little water if needed to achieve a dal consistency.

Garnish with the chopped coriander and serve with rice or chapatis.

EASY DAL

LACHKO DAL

GF

This recipe could not be simpler! Healthy and packed with flavour and protein, this is a dish for tired (and overworked!) parents – and children love it. In fact, I prepared a milder version of this dish for my own babies when they were toddlers. For the adults, you may enjoy this with Mango Pickle (page 46) to enhance the flavour. It is delicious when mixed with rice.

We actually call this dish 'pooka-style dal' at home, the nickname for our youngest daughter Ravina.

Serves 4
Prep time: 10 minutes
Cook time: 35 minutes

90g/3¼oz/½ cup dried split pigeon peas (toor dal)

480ml/16fl oz/2 cups water

1 tbsp oil

½ tsp mustard seeds

pinch of asafoetida

2 dried red chillies

½ tsp ground turmeric

¾ tsp chilli powder

salt, to taste

1 tbsp ghee, to finish

rice, to serve

Wash the split pigeon peas under cold, running water until the water runs clear. Place the rinsed pigeon peas in a pressure cooker along with the water (see Note if not using a pressure cooker). Secure the lid and cook under full pressure for 20 minutes. Lower the heat and simmer for another 10 minutes. Allow the pressure cooker to decompress before safely removing the lid. Set aside.

Heat the oil in a medium-sized pan and add the mustard seeds. Once the seeds begin to crackle, add the asafoetida, whole dried chillies and the cooked dal, along with the ground turmeric, chilli powder and salt. Cook over a low heat for 3–4 minutes, adjusting the consistency with 60ml/2fl oz/¼ cup water if necessary.

Top with the ghee and serve with rice.

Note: If not using a pressure cooker, place the rinsed peas in a deep saucepan and cover with 1.4 litres/48fl oz/6 cups hot water. Leave to soak for 4 hours. Bring the peas and soaking water to the boil, skimming off froth as needed. Cover and cook over a medium heat for 1½ hours until the peas are very mushy.

GUJARATI DAL

GF   DF   VG

One of my sisters taught me how to make this Gujarati dish, and this is my version. Traditionally served at events such as weddings and baby showers, I am taken back to all those wonderful celebrations whenever I serve it. My beloved father was a *huge* fan of my dal, and I only wish that I could send it to him now. This recipe is a tribute to a successful businessman and a loving father. You are in my prayers, Jay Shree Ambe!

If you don't have a pressure cooker, see the Note on page 117.

Serves 4
Prep time: 15 minutes
Cook time: 35–40 minutes

60g/2oz/⅓ cup dried split pigeon peas (toor dal)

85g/3oz/½ cup chopped tomatoes

3 tbsp grated jaggery (gur)

2½ tsp fresh lime juice

½ tsp ground turmeric

1½ tsp Coriander-cumin Powder (page 29)

¾ tsp salt, or to taste

For the seasoning
2 tbsp oil

1 tsp mustard seeds

pinch of asafoetida

1½ tsp Kashmiri chilli powder

1 tsp Pickle Masala (page 34)

3 tbsp chopped coriander (cilantro)

dried chillies, to garnish (optional)

rice or Roti (page 168), to serve

Wash the pigeon peas under cold, running water three times. Place the rinsed peas in a pressure cooker along with 700ml/24fl oz/3 cups water. Secure the lid and cook under full pressure for 20–25 minutes. Allow the pressure cooker to decompress before safely removing the lid. Allow the mixture to cool slightly before blending to a mushy and smooth mixture and whisking well.

Transfer the cooked dal into a deep saucepan, add the tomatoes, jaggery, lime juice, ground turmeric, coriander-cumin powder, salt and 125ml/4fl oz/½ cup water. Mix well and bring to the boil, then reduce the heat to medium and simmer for 8 minutes, stirring regularly.

For the seasoning, heat the oil in a small frying pan or skillet and add the mustard seeds. Once they begin to crackle, add the asafoetida. Cook for 2 seconds and add the chilli powder, then immediately pour the seasoning over the dal.

Stir the pickle masala and chopped coriander into the dal and cook for 3–4 minutes over a low heat. Add a little water, if needed, to loosen.

Garnish with dried chillies, if using, and serve with rice or roti.

Note: Adding chilli powder to the hot oil just gives some red colour to the dal, but you need to work quickly before the chilli powder turns black in the hot oil.

SAMOSA SOUP

DF

Serves 4
Prep time: 15 minutes
Cook time: 65–75 minutes

In this soup I take a much-loved and popular snack and merge it with the sweet, spicy and sour notes of Burmese cuisine. It turned out to be a lifesaver when one of my daughters suffered heavily from allergies one year. She happily devoured it for lunch and supper for six months straight! If there are any leftovers, even better, because it's fantastic the next day.

45g/1½oz/¼ cup dried split pigeon peas (toor dal)

2 tbsp oil

1 tsp cumin seeds

3 dried red chillies

1 green chilli, stem removed and slit in half

140g/5oz/1 cup thinly sliced red onion

¼ tsp freshly ground black pepper

1 tbsp ground coriander

½ tsp ground turmeric

2 tsp Kashmiri chilli powder

1 tsp garam masala

1.2 litres/40fl oz/5 cups vegetable stock

100g/3½oz/¾ cup cooked chickpeas (garbanzo beans) or canned chickpeas, rinsed

2 tsp Tamarind Purée (page 36) or fresh lime juice

salt, to taste

20g/¾oz/½ cup chopped coriander

12 frozen cocktail-sized or 4 homemade samosas (page 102)

50g/1¾oz/½ cup chopped spring onions (scallions), to garnish

Wash the pigeon peas under cold, running water three time. Place the rinsed peas in a pressure cooker along with 240ml/8fl oz/1 cup water. Secure the lid and cook under full pressure for 20–25 minutes. Allow the pressure cooker to decompress before safely removing the lid. Set aside.

Heat the oil in a saucepan over a medium heat and add the cumin seeds. Once they begin to crackle, add the dried red chillies, green chilli and red onion and cook for 12–15 minutes over a medium-low heat until the onions soften and caramelize. Add the black pepper along with the ground coriander, ground turmeric, chilli powder and garam masala. Mix well and cook for 1 minute. Pour in the stock and add the chickpeas, the dal and the tamarind purée. Cook over a medium-low heat for 30 minutes. Add salt to taste and half the coriander (cilantro) and cook for 2–3 minutes.

If using frozen samosas, cook the samosas according to the package instructions. Divide the pieces between 4 warm soup bowls. Ladle the soup into the bowls and serve garnished with the remaining coriander and the spring onions.

Note: If not using a pressure cooker, place the rinsed peas in a deep saucepan and cover with 1–1.4 litres/32–48fl oz/4–6 cups hot water. Leave to soak for 4 hours. Bring the peas and soaking water to the boil, skimming off froth as needed. Cover and cook over a medium heat for 1½ hours until the peas are very mushy.

SPICY GARLIC SOUP

GARLIC RASAM

Serves 4
Prep time: 10 minutes
Cook time: 25–30 minutes

For the rasam powder
¼ tsp ghee

1 tbsp dried split pigeon peas
  (toor dal)

1 tbsp coriander seeds

½ tsp black peppercorns

½ tsp cumin seeds

6–8 fresh curry leaves

1 dried red chilli

For the rasam
1 large tomato, chopped

5–6 fresh curry leaves

pinch of asafoetida

salt, to taste

700ml/24fl oz/3 cups water

90g/3¼oz/½ cup cooked split
  pigeon peas (toor dal)

1 tsp Tamarind Purée (page 36)

For the seasoning
1 tbsp ghee, plus 1 tbsp to serve

1 tsp mustard seeds

3 garlic cloves, crushed

2 dried red chillies

6–8 fresh curry leaves

To finish
10g/⅓oz/¼ cup chopped
  coriander (cilantro)

This unique rasam recipe happens to be a favourite for many reasons. The dominant flavour of the crushed garlic used in the seasoning and the ghee added at the end enhances the overall taste of this light and healthy dish. Many would say that this soup is perfect for soothing a sore throat in the winter months (thanks to the medicinal properties of the spices), but I would argue it's perfect all year round. I love the South Indian flavours of this wonderful soup and I would love you to try this one.

For the rasam powder, melt the ghee in a small pan over a medium-low heat and add the rest of the ingredients, cooking for 4–6 minutes until roasted golden and fragrant. Remove from the heat and allow to cool slightly before grinding to a powder using a grinder. Set aside.

To make the rasam, place the chopped tomato, curry leaves, asafoetida, salt and rasam powder in a medium saucepan along with 240ml/8fl oz/1 cup of the water. Mix well and cook over a medium heat until the tomato has cooked down, approximately 10 minutes. Stir in the cooked dal and tamarind purée and add the remaining 460ml/16fl oz/2 cups of water. Cook for 8–10 minutes and remove the pan from the heat.

For the seasoning, heat the ghee in a small pan and add the mustard seeds. Once they begin to crackle, add the garlic, dried chillies and curry leaves. Cook until the garlic partially caramelizes, then remove the pan from the heat and immediately pour the seasoning on top of the rasam. Garnish with the coriander and the extra tablespoon of ghee. Serve with rice, if you like.

CLASSIC GUJARATI: LEGUMES (KATHOL)

Protein-rich dried beans, or pulses, are called kathol in Gujarati. Because our diets are largely vegetarian, the dried beans provided us with a great source of protein needed for a balanced diet. When dried beans are processed and their skins removed, we call them dals (for example, mung dal, chana dal, toor dal, etc.).

Dals can be prepared on their own, but we also enjoy them in curried dishes and generally serve them with rice. To prepare the dried beans, I highly recommend you to soak them for a good 6–8 hours so that they are softened and ready to be cooked.

SPICED YOGURT SOUP
GUJARATI KADHI

GF   Q

Kadhi holds a very special place in my heart (and my kitchen) and I am thrilled to share this recipe with you. It is inspired by feedback and input from several family members – as well as the friendly owner of a popular restaurant in Vadodara.

A kadhi is a simple dish of yogurt thickened with gram flour (besan), full of flavour and very healthy. It is often served as a lunch option in Gujarat along with rice, chapatis or the puffed, deep-fried bread known as poori. The recipe calls for Indian bay leaf (tamal patra), but a regular bay leaf can be used in a pinch.

Serves 3
Prep time: 10 minutes
Cook time: 20 minutes

160g/5¾oz/¾ cup plain full-fat yogurt

1 tbsp gram flour (besan)

700ml/24fl oz/3 cups water

2 tbsp grated jaggery (gur) or sugar

1 tbsp Ginger Paste (page 32)

1 tbsp plus 1 tsp Green Chilli Paste (page 32)

¾ tsp salt, or to taste

1½ tbsp ghee

¾ tsp cumin seeds

2 dried red chillies

10–12 fresh curry leaves

¼ tsp asafoetida

1 tbsp roughly chopped garlic scapes (optional)

1 Indian bay leaf (tamal patra)

3 tbsp chopped coriander (cilantro), to garnish

rice, chapatis or Pooris (page 167), to serve

Combine the yogurt and gram flour in a large saucepan. Whisk until very smooth (this is important), then stir in the water until smooth. Add the jaggery, ginger paste, green chilli paste and salt. (The ginger may cause the mixture to split, but it'll fix itself once it's cooked.)

In a small frying pan or skillet, heat the ghee over a medium heat. Add the cumin seeds. Once the seeds begin to pop, add the dried red chillies, curry leaves and asafoetida. Mix well and cook for 5–7 seconds. Add this mixture to the yogurt-gram flour mixture and stir well to combine. Bring the mixture to the boil, then immediately reduce the heat to low. Cook for 20–22 minutes. Add the garlic scapes, if using, and the bay leaf and garnish with the coriander.

Serve with rice, chapatis or pooris.

CURRIES

CAULIFLOWER AND POTATO NU SHAAK

GF   DF   VG   Q

As a mother, nothing gives me more pleasure than cooking for my children and sharing meals with my family. My elder daughter is particularly fond of this dish and when we travel to India it's all she wants.

Thankfully, I have taught my husband how to make it (up to my daughter's high standards) if ever I am away from home. We serve it with chapatis and enjoy it with some rice or dal (or a combination of both).

Serves 4–5
Prep time: 5 minutes
Cook time: 25 minutes

5–6 tbsp oil

1½ tsp mustard seeds

¼ tsp asafoetida

2 potatoes, peeled and cut into 2cm (¾-inch) cubes

1 cauliflower, patted dry and cut into 2cm (¾-inch) florets

1½ tsp ground turmeric

1 tbsp chilli powder

1 tbsp Coriander-cumin Powder (page 29)

1½ tsp sugar

salt, to taste

chapatis, to serve

Heat the oil in a large frying pan or skillet and add the mustard seeds. Once they begin to crackle, add the asafoetida and potatoes. Cook for 2 minutes. Add the cauliflower florets, stirring well to coat evenly.

Add the ground turmeric, chilli powder and coriander-cumin powder. Partially cover the pan with a lid and continue to cook over a low heat for 20 minutes, stirring occasionally to avoid the vegetables sticking to the bottom. Uncover the pan and cook for a further 4–6 minutes.

Remove the pan from the heat once the potatoes and cauliflower florets have cooked through. Stir in the sugar and season to taste with salt.

Serve with chapatis.

GREEN PEPPER AND BESAN MASALA

BESAN MURCHA NU SHAAK

GF   DF   VG   Q

This simple recipe requires only a handful of ingredients and less than 15 minutes to make. Moreish and memorable, this is my mother's special recipe and therefore one of my favourite dishes. Only she knows how to make it just like a mom can – perfectly! Thanks, Mom, for the lovely recipe.

Bursting with exotic flavours, it is most delicious when served with chapatis. I hope you will experience the same love for this recipe as I do.

Serves 4
Prep time: 5 minutes
Cook time: 10 minutes

125g/4½oz/½ cup gram flour (besan)

3½ tbsp oil

1 tsp ajwain (carom) seeds

¼ tsp asafoetida

1 large green bell pepper, roughly chopped

salt, to taste

¼ tsp ground turmeric

1½ tsp chilli powder

2 tsp Coriander-cumin Powder (page 29)

1 tsp sugar

chapatis, Roti (page 168) or Bhakhri (page 166), to serve

Roast the gram flour in a small, dry frying pan or skillet over a medium heat for 2–3 minutes. Remove from the heat and set aside.

In a second, larger pan, heat the oil. Add the ajwain seeds and cook until they begin to crackle. Add the asafoetida, chopped bell pepper and a little salt and cook for 2 minutes over a medium heat, stirring occasionally. Add the turmeric, chilli powder and the coriander-cumin powder and cook for 1 minute. Add the roasted gram flour to the pan along with 1–2 tablespoons of water and mix in well. Cook for another 2 minutes before stirring in the sugar, then remove the pan from the heat.

Serve warm with chapatis, roti or bhakhri.

PAN-FRIED AUBERGINE CURRY WITH YOGURT

ACHARI BAINGAN

GF

Serves 4
Prep time: 10 minutes +
1 hour draining
Cook time: 20 minutes

I am often asked to give cooking lessons, and nothing beats the joy I feel when sharing my food. I know many who don't like the taste of aubergine (eggplant), and then thoroughly enjoy this dish when I make it for them. This humble vegetable is low in calories, rich in nutrients, and high in fibre and antioxidants.

4–6 baby aubergines (eggplants)

2 tsp salt

125ml/4fl oz/½ cup oil

For the curry

3 tbsp oil

1 tsp mustard seeds

pinch of asafoetida

½ tsp nigella (black onion) seeds

½ tsp fenugreek seeds

2 tsp Ginger Paste (page 32)

200g/7oz/1¼ cups finely chopped ripe tomatoes

1½ tbsp Spice Blend (page 139)

1½ tsp chilli powder

½ tsp ground turmeric

70g/2½oz/⅓ cup plain full-fat yogurt

3 tbsp double (heavy) cream

chopped coriander (cilantro)

Roti (page 168) or Parathas (page 174), to serve

Wash the aubergines and trim off and discard the stems. Cut each into 4 wedges. Lay the pieces in a colander, scatter over the salt and mix well. Set aside for 1 hour to drain the released moisture. Rinse the pieces thoroughly with cold water and pat dry with paper towels.

Heat the oil in a deep pan over a medium heat and pan-fry the aubergines for 5–7 minutes, until cooked through. Transfer to a plate and set aside.

To make the curry, heat the oil in a saucepan over a medium heat. Add the mustard seeds, and once they begin to crackle, add the asafoetida, nigella seeds and fenugreek seeds and cook over a medium heat for 20 seconds. Add the ginger paste, chopped tomatoes, spice blend, chilli powder and ground turmeric and a little salt to taste. Mix well and cook for 5 minutes, stirring occasionally. Add the yogurt and 125ml/4fl oz/½ cup water to the mixture and mix well. Add the pan-fried aubergines and mix again. Turn the heat to low, stir in the cream and cook for another 5 minutes.

Transfer the aubergine curry to a serving dish, garnish with coriander and serve with roti or parathas, if you like.

GARLIC AND POTATO CURRY
LASANIYA BATATA

GF   DF   VG

Serves 4
Prep time: 15 minutes +
20 minutes soaking
Cook time: 50–60 minutes

One of my family's favourite destinations when visiting Gujarat is a restaurant in Vadodara. After befriending the owner, he kindly shared this recipe with me. Kathiyawadi food is less sweet than other Gujarati regional cuisines, with generous use of garlic and chillies. Use dried Kashmiri chillies, if you can.

For the red chilli paste

6–7 dried red chillies

5 garlic cloves

1 tomato

For the potatoes

10 unpeeled baby potatoes
    (or 3 medium, quartered)

2 tsp oil, plus 3 tbsp to finish

1 tsp chaat powder

To finish

½ tsp mustard seeds

¾ tsp cumin seeds

¼ tsp asafoetida

90g/3¼oz/¾ cup finely chopped
    red onion

50g/1¾oz/½ cup chopped spring
    onion (scallion)

3 tbsp chopped garlic scapes
    (optional)

¼ tsp ground turmeric

½ tsp garam masala

1 tsp Kashmiri chilli powder

1 tsp Coriander-cumin Powder
    (page 29)

3 tbsp chopped coriander
    (cilantro), to garnish

For the chilli paste, start by removing the seeds from the dried chillies. This can easily be done by simply using kitchen scissors to slice the tops off and tapping out (and discarding) as many seeds as possible (if using Kashmiri chillies, just slice the tops off – no need to remove the seeds). Place the deseeded chillies in 125ml/4fl oz/½ cup hot water and leave to soak for 20 minutes. Drain and blitz them in a mini food processor along with the garlic, tomato and 1–2 tablespoons water. Once you have achieved a smooth paste, set aside.

Boil the potatoes for 15–20 minutes or until tender. Drain and leave until cool enough to handle then peel off the skins. Heat the 2 teaspoons of oil in a pan and add the chaat powder. Add the peeled potatoes and mix well to coat in the oil. Cook for 20–30 seconds, stirring continuously. Remove the pan from the heat and allow the potatoes to marinate while you finish the curry.

Heat the 3 tablespoons of oil in a saucepan and add the mustard seeds. When they start to crackle, add the cumin seeds and the asafoetida, then the red chilli paste. Cover the pan and cook over a low heat for 6–7 minutes, stirring occasionally. Add the red onion, spring onion and garlic scapes, if using, and cook for 18–20 minutes until the onions soften. Next add the ground turmeric, garam masala, chilli powder, coriander-cumin powder and some salt to taste (about ¾ tsp). Cook for another 5 minutes, while stirring. Tip in the marinated potatoes and add 185ml/6fl oz/¾ cup water. Cook for another 8–10 minutes over a medium-low heat. Add a little more water if needed to achieve your desired consistency.

Garnish with the chopped coriander, and roasted chillies and garlic, if you like. Serve with chapatis.

POTATO AND PEA CURRY
ALOO MUTTER IN GRAVY

GF   DF   VG   Q

There is a very special story behind this dish and I simply must share it. It was one of the first dishes I ever learnt to make (I like to call it the Bachelor's Dish!) and one of very few I had in my culinary arsenal when I got married and moved to the States. I was an inexperienced cook and served it to my husband's friends for dinner one night along with fresh hand-rolled roti. I watched them wolf it down, thinking it was typical of hungry young men – but later realized they truly *loved* it! I shared the recipe with them and was (and still am) delighted to hear they often make it for their families. As a tradition, I serve it every time they visit us, some thirty years later. I love how food connects people, creating lifelong friendships.

Serves 4
Prep time: 10 minutes
Cook time: 15 minutes

3 tbsp oil

¾ tsp cumin seeds, slightly crushed or roughly ground

pinch of asafoetida

½ tsp ground turmeric

1½ tsp chilli powder

570ml/20fl oz/2½ cups water

2 potatoes, peeled and cut into 2cm (¾-inch) cubes

250g/9oz/2 cups shelled petits pois or peas, thawed if frozen

1½ tsp Coriander-cumin Powder (page 29)

¾ tsp Garlic Paste (page 31)

salt, to taste

3 tbsp chopped coriander (cilantro)

1 tbsp chopped garlic scapes (optional)

Roti (page 168), to serve

Heat the oil in a deep saucepan over a medium heat and add the cumin seeds. Once they begin to crackle, add the asafoetida, ground turmeric, chilli powder and water. Bring to the boil, then add the potatoes, peas, coriander-cumin powder, garlic paste, and salt to taste. Cover partially with a lid and cook for 12–14 minutes over a medium heat. Uncover the pan and add the chopped coriander. Reduce the heat to low and cook for another 2 minutes, stirring occasionally. Add another 60ml/2fl oz/¼ cup of water if needed.

Stir in the chopped garlic scapes, if using, and remove the pan from the heat. Serve with roti.

SMOKY AUBERGINE
RINGAN NO ODO

GF DF VG

Sometimes the best recipes are discovered between two friends who share the love of food and cooking. This particular recipe (known in Punjabi as baingan bharta, similar to Gujarati ringan no odo) was sent to me by a special friend via text after we discussed it at length, but she provided no quantities or instructions, only a list of ingredients. The next day, I made it myself and changed a few elements and now I love it even more!

Trying this out myself boosted my confidence in the kitchen and made me realize that learning by my senses taught me to be a better cook. I hope you enjoy it as much as I do.

Serves 4
Prep time: 10 minutes
Cook time: 1 hour 20 minutes

1 large aubergine (eggplant)

60ml/2fl oz/¼ cup olive oil, plus extra for brushing

145g/5½oz/1¼ cups chopped onion

4–5 small ripe tomatoes, chopped

2 tbsp finely chopped green chilli

10g/⅓oz/¼ cup chopped coriander (cilantro), plus extra to garnish

salt, to taste

Roti (page 168), naan or chapatis, to serve

Preheat the grill (broiler) to high.

Brush the aubergine with oil and pierce the skin 2–3 times with a fork. Wrap the aubergine in foil and grill for 22 minutes. Turn the aubergine and grill the other side for 20 minutes. (Alternatively, put the foil-wrapped aubergine on a baking sheet in a preheated oven at 200°C fan/220°C/425°F/gas mark 7 and bake for 1 hour.) Allow to cool then remove the foil. Halve the aubergine and scoop out the cooked flesh into a small bowl. Mash the flesh and set aside.

Heat the oil in a pan over a medium heat and add the onion. Turn the heat to low and cook the onions for 20 minutes until they have softened and are light brown in colour. Add the tomatoes and green chilli and cook for 5 minutes. Once the tomatoes and green chillies have cooked down, stir in the mashed aubergine and chopped coriander and season with salt. Cook over a low heat for another 8–10 minutes.

Garnish with the extra coriander. Excellent with roti, naan or chapatis.

SPICED SCRAMBLED EGGS

EGG BHURJI

GF   Q

The first time I told my kids I was going to make this dish, they all scoffed and dismissed it. I told them I would make it anyway and they had at least to try it. They enjoyed it so much that now we often have it for breakfast. It just goes to show that you should try everything once – the results may just surprise you. The secret to the recipe? The pav bhaji masala. This beautiful masala can be found at any Indian supermarket. There are many types but if you can get Bombay pav bhaji masala, I like that best for this recipe.

Serves 4
Prep time: 5 minutes
Cook time: 20 minutes

4 tbsp butter

½ tsp cumin seeds

85g/3oz/¾ cup chopped red onion

1½ tsp pav bhaji masala, preferably Bombay

1 tsp chilli powder

½ tsp ground turmeric

1½ tsp finely chopped green chilli

120g/4¼oz/¾ cup chopped tomatoes

1 tsp Garlic Paste (page 31)

¾ tsp salt, to taste

6 eggs, well beaten

2 tbsp chopped spring onions (scallions), optional

15g/½oz/½ cup rocket (arugula) leaves, to garnish

dinner rolls or pav, to serve

Heat the butter in a frying pan or skillet over a medium heat and add the cumin seeds. Once the seeds start to crackle, add the red onion and cook for 10 minutes, or until the onions have softened. Add the pav bhaji masala, chilli powder and ground turmeric and cook for 2 minutes.

Add the chopped green chilli, tomatoes, garlic paste and salt and cook for 4–5 minutes, stirring regularly. Add the eggs and cook for 3–4 minutes, stirring continuously until the eggs have scrambled.

Gently stir in the spring onions, if using, and garnish with the rocket leaves. Delicious with dinner rolls or pav.

CAULIFLOWER WITH CURRY LEAVES

GF   DF   VG

Serves 4
Prep time: 10 minutes
Cook time: 40–45 minutes

A family friend (originally from Andrapradesh) came to our home one day and taught me how to make this simple cauliflower curry. It is now a firm family favourite, especially with my daughter, who often requests it when she comes home. The homemade spice blend and the fresh curry leaves make all the difference – you should be able to find the leaves in larger supermarkets.

For the spice blend

2 cloves

2 green cardamom pods

2 tbsp coriander seeds

¼ tsp cumin seeds

¼ tsp broken cinnamon stick

For the curry and seasoning

1 large onion, chopped

1 tsp ground turmeric

1 green chilli, stem removed and sliced in half lengthways

2 tsp Garlic Paste (page 31)

1 tsp Ginger Paste (page 32)

2 tbsp Spice Blend (see above)

1 cauliflower (about 500g/18oz), cut into 4cm (1½-inch) florets

3 tbsp oil

1 tsp mustard seeds

10–12 fresh curry leaves

2 dried red chillies

1½ tsp chilli powder

salt, to taste

chopped coriander (cilantro), to garnish

rice, to serve

For the spice blend, blitz all the ingredients to a fine powder and set aside.

Bring 700ml/24fl oz/3 cups of water to the boil in a large saucepan. Add the onion, turmeric, green chilli, the garlic and ginger pastes and ½ tablespoon of the spice blend. Cook over a medium-high heat for 25–30 minutes. Add the cauliflower, reduce the heat to medium and cook, partially covered, for 8 minutes, until the cauliflower is tender.

When the cauliflower is nearly cooked, make the seasoning. Heat the oil in a frying pan or skillet over a medium heat and add the mustard seeds. Once they begin to crackle, add the curry leaves, red chillies, chilli powder and remaining spice blend, then immediately add the seasoning to the pan of cauliflower and mix well. Reduce the heat to low and cook for 3–4 minutes until the sauce has thickened. Add a little more water if needed.

Season with salt and garnish with coriander. Serve with rice.

Note: Leftover spice blend can be stored in an airtight container for up to 6 months.

INDIAN BEANS IN GREEN CURRY

SURTI LILVA NU SHAK

GF   DF   VG   Q

Surti lilva is a type of bean widely used in Gujarati cooking as they boast a variety of healthy nutrients. They are also beautifully bright and simply perfect for this green curry. I ate this dish at a roadside restaurant (known as a dhaba) in north Gujarat and was thrilled when the owner described the dish to me and explained how it is made. I was even more thrilled when my first attempt at it was spot on. I am forever grateful to him for sharing this delicious recipe with me – and I can now share it with you.

If you are using fresh lilva, shell the surti papdi pod and use only the beans. Alternatively, frozen surti lilva are easily found in Indian stores. If neither is available, you can use frozen butter (lima) beans.

Serves 4
Prep time: 5 minutes
Cook time: 20 minutes

4 tbsp groundnut (peanut) oil

1 tsp ajwain (carom) seeds

pinch of asafoetida

110g/3¾oz/½ cup Green Paste, plus extra to garnish (page 30)

300g/10½oz/2 cups surti lilva or baby butter (lima) beans, thawed if frozen

2 tsp Coriander-cumin Powder (page 29)

salt, to taste

350ml/12fl oz/1½ cups water

2 tsp sugar

3 tbsp finely chopped coriander (cilantro)

2 tbsp finely chopped garlic scapes (optional)

roasted chilli, to garnish (optional)

Bhakhri (page 166) or Roti (page 168), to serve

Heat the oil in a pressure cooker over a medium heat. Add the ajwain seeds and once they begin to crackle, add the asafoetida. Reduce the heat to low and add the green paste and cook for 2 minutes, stirring constantly.

Add the surti lilva or butter beans, coriander-cumin powder and salt along with the water. Secure the lid of the pressure cooker and cook for 15 minutes. Allow the pressure cooker to decompress before safely removing the lid. You may need to add another 60ml/2fl oz/¼ cup of water to achieve the right consistency. Mix it well.

Stir in the sugar, coriander and garlic scapes, if using, and mix well. Garnish with green paste and the roasted chilli, if using. Serve with bhakhri or roti.

Note: If not using a pressure cooker, prepare step 1 of the recipe in a saucepan. Add the surti lilva, coriander-cumin powder and salt along with 700ml/24fl oz/3 cups hot water. Partially cover with a lid and cook over a medium-low heat for 1 hour, until the surti lilva are very tender.

EASY-PEASY POTATO CURRY
SUKHI BHAJI

GF   DF   VG

Serves 4
Prep time: 10 minutes
Cook time: 25–30 minutes

This is one of the tastiest and simplest dry curries one could make. We garnish it with fresh garlic scapes, which truly enhance the flavour. I haven't forgotten my Gujarati roots, and made sure there was an element of sweet (sugar) and sour (lime) in this lovely dish. Enjoy!

4 potatoes

3 tbsp oil

1 tsp mustard seeds

¼ tsp asafoetida

4–5 dried red chillies

10–12 fresh curry leaves

85g/3oz/¾ cup chopped red onion

3 tbsp whole cashew nuts

40g/1½oz/⅓ cup podded fresh or frozen peas, thawed if frozen

¾ tsp ground turmeric

2–3 tsp Green Chilli Paste (page 32)

1½ tsp Coriander-cumin Powder (page 29)

1 tsp salt, or to taste

1 tsp fresh lime juice

1½ tsp sugar

To finish
1 tbsp chopped coriander (cilantro)

1 tbsp chopped garlic scapes (optional)

chapatis, to serve

Boil the potatoes in a pan of water for 15–20 minutes. Once tender, drain and allow to cool. Peel the potatoes and dice into 2cm (¾-inch) cubes. Set aside.

Heat the oil in a large pan and add the mustard seeds. Once they begin to crackle, add the asafoetida, dried chillies, curry leaves, onion and cashews. Cook for 6–7 minutes over a medium heat, stirring occasionally. Add the peas and cook until tender. Add the ground turmeric, green chilli paste, coriander-cumin powder and salt, along with the cooked potatoes. Cook for 4–5 minutes. Add 2 tablespoons water if needed.

Remove the pan from the heat and stir in the lime juice and sugar. Garnish with the chopped coriander and garlic scapes, if using, and serve with chapatis.

AMRITSARI CHOLE

GF

Serves 4
Prep time: 10 minutes +
6–8 hours soaking
Cook time: 50 minutes

170g/6oz/1 cup dried chickpeas
  (garbanzo beans)

700ml/24fl oz/3 cups cold water

1 black tea bag, tag removed

1 tsp salt

60g/2oz/¼ cup ghee

½ tsp cumin seeds

120g/4¼oz/1 cup finely chopped
  red onion

¼ tsp ground turmeric

1–1½ tsp chilli powder

1½ tsp Garlic Paste (page 31)

2½ tsp Punjabi chole masala
  or 2 tsp garam masala

165g/5½oz/¾ cup Tomato Purée
  (page 36)

2 tbsp chopped coriander
  (cilantro), to garnish

To serve
Pooris (page 167)

60g/2oz/⅓–½ cup thinly sliced
  red onion

Mango Pickle (page 46)

Amritsari chole is widely appreciated throughout north India and is served in eateries and by street vendors alike. Chole is a type of chickpea curry that we serve with pooris. It is most often served with mango pickle and red onions. While the dish itself can be oily, my version is healthier, less greasy and still uncompromised on flavour. Punjabi chole masala is my preferred masala for this recipe and is available in Indian supermarkets.

Place the chickpeas in a bowl and cover with the cold water. Leave to soak for 6–8 hours, but preferably overnight.

Put the chickpeas and their soaking water into a pressure cooker along with the tea bag and salt. Secure the lid and cook under full pressure for 7–8 minutes, then turn the heat to low and cook for 30 minutes until the beans are tender. Allow the pressure cooker to decompress before safely removing the lid. Remove and discard the tea bag and set the beans aside.

Melt the ghee in a saucepan over a medium heat and add the cumin seeds. When the seeds start to crackle, add the chopped red onion and cook for 20 minutes over a low heat or until the onion has softened, stirring regularly. Add the turmeric, chilli powder, garlic paste and Punjabi chole masala or garam masala and cook for 8 minutes. Stir in the tomato purée and cook for 4–5 minutes. Add the cooked chickpeas and their cooking water. Cook for 15 minutes over a medium-low heat.

Use the back of a spoon to mash a portion of the mixture. Add 60–125ml/2–4fl oz/¼–½ cup water and mix well. Add the chopped coriander and remove the pan from the heat. Serve with pooris, red onion slices and mango pickle.

Note: If not using a pressure cooker, place the chickpeas in a deep saucepan and cover with 1.65 litres/56fl oz/7 cups hot water. Leave to soak overnight. Bring the chickpeas and soaking water to the boil, removing as much froth as possible from the surface. Add the tea bag and salt, then partially cover with a lid and cook over a medium heat for 1¼ hours until the chickpeas are tender. Add more water, if needed, for a thick curry consistency.

CURRIED RUNNER BEANS WITH FENUGREEK DUMPLINGS

VALOR MUTHIA NU SHAAK

DF VG

Serves 4–5
Prep time: 20 minutes
Cook time: 1 hr 15 minutes

For the paste
2 tbsp grated fresh coconut

10g/⅓oz/¼ cup chopped
   coriander (cilantro)

3 garlic cloves

2 tbsp peanuts

2.5cm (1-inch) piece of fresh
   ginger, peeled

2 green chillies, stems removed

salt, to taste

For the fenugreek dumplings
60g/2oz/½ cup gram flour (besan)

100g/3½oz/¾ cup wholemeal
   (wholewheat) flour

½ tsp ground turmeric

pinch of asafoetida

½ tsp garam masala

1 tbsp Green Chilli Paste (page 32)

1½ tsp Ginger Paste (page 32)

1 tsp Coriander-cumin Powder
   (page 29)

2 tsp sugar

1 tsp lime juice

¾ tsp salt, or to taste

½ bunch fenugreek leaves (methi
   leaves), roots removed and
   chopped (about 28g/1oz/1 cup)

This dish has fast-tracked to becoming one of my favourite recipes of all time. Featuring curried runner beans with fenugreek dumplings (known as muthia), it is a Gujarati dish appreciated by my wide circle of Indian friends. It takes a little more effort than most of my other recipes, which is exactly why you should put in that extra bit of work and serve it at your next dinner party. Your friends and families will love it and you will be tempted to make this all the time.

Combine all the ingredients for the paste in a blender or food processor and blend to a coarse consistency. Add 1–2 tablespoons of water if needed and set aside.

To make the dumplings, combine all the ingredients in a bowl with 2–3 tablespoons of water and mix well until it forms dough. Divide the dough into 14–16 equal-sized portions and shape into balls.

Heat the oil for frying in a deep saucepan on a medium heat. Working in batches to avoid overcrowding, add a few dumplings to the pan and deep-fry for 3–4 minutes, until golden. Using a metal slotted spoon or skimmer, move them around to ensure even cooking. Remove with the slotted spoon and place on paper towels to absorb excess grease while you cook the rest.

For the vegetables, trim and discard the strings from the valor papdi. (It is a good idea to open up the pods and check for hidden worms and remove them.) Open each pod, cut into 2.5cm (1-inch) pieces and set aside.

Heat 3 tablespoons of oil in a wok. Add the ajwain seeds and asafoetida. Once the seeds begin to crackle, add the valor papdi along with 750ml/26fl oz/3¼ cups water. Add the prepared paste, ground turmeric, coriander-cumin powder, chilli powder and some salt. Mix well. Cover and cook for 50 minutes.

10g/⅓oz/¼ cup chopped coriander
(cilantro), plus 2 tbsp to garnish

3 tbsp oil, plus 700–950ml/24–
32fl oz/3–4 cups for deep-frying

For the vegetables
450g/1lb fresh or frozen valor
papdi or runner beans, thawed
if frozen

¾ tsp ajwain (carom) seeds

½ tsp asafoetida

pinch of ground turmeric

1 tbsp Coriander-cumin Powder
(page 29)

½ tsp chilli powder

1 tsp sugar

Place the fried dumplings on top of the mixture. Add 120ml/4fl oz/
½ cup water, cover, and cook for another 5–10 minutes. Stir in the
sugar, mix gently and garnish with the extra chopped coriander.

Serve with roti (page 168).

CASHEW CURRY

KAJU CURRY MASALA

GF

I have many fond memories of my college years, but none more so than kaju curry. I was always trying to track down the tastiest dishes, which is tricky when you are a student on a budget! Imagine my delight when I stumbled upon a restaurant across the road from my university and tried this curry. My attempts at getting them to share the recipe didn't work out (understandably, due to their company policy), but it did increase my curiosity and helped me develop a new skill for creating a recipe from memory. After much development and testing, I can share with you what I believe to be an even better version than I enjoyed back then. When I created my final, perfected version my kids devoured it two days in a row! It just goes to show what a bit of persistence can do...

Serves 4
Prep time: 10 minutes
Cook time: 50 minutes

60ml/2fl oz/¼ cup oil

1 onion, chopped

2 tsp chilli powder

½ tsp ground turmeric

350g/12oz/1½ cups Tomato Purée (page 36)

1 tbsp Garlic Paste (page 31)

¾ tsp garam masala

1½ tsp Coriander-cumin Powder (page 29)

60ml/2fl oz/¼ cup double (heavy) cream, plus extra to serve

60g/2oz/¼ cup Cashew Paste (page 35)

salt, to taste

60g/2oz/½ cup store-bought roasted cashew nuts

1 tbsp chopped coriander (cilantro), to garnish

Roti (page 168), to serve

Heat the oil in wok over a medium-low heat and add the onion, cooking for 20 minutes. Add the chilli powder and ground turmeric and cook for 2–3 minutes. Tip in the tomato purée and stir well before adding the garlic paste. Cook for 5 minutes, then add the garam masala and cook for another 3 minutes. Add the coriander-cumin powder and cook over a very low heat for 10 minutes, stirring gently. Pour in the cream and cook for 8 minutes until the fat visibly rises to the surface. If necessary, add 125ml/4fl oz/½ cup water. Stir in the cashew paste and cook for 2 minutes.

Season the mixture with salt and scatter over the cashew nuts. Do not stir the mixture again, but simply garnish with the chopped coriander and a little cream and enjoy with roti.

CLUSTER BEANS WITH SESAME SEEDS

GAWAR NU SHAAK

GF   DF   VG   Q

Cluster beans, which look like a thicker version of green beans, are high in fibre and this homely dish makes a satisfying vegetarian meal. It can be served with dal and rice; curd and raita; or, my personal favourite, Bhakhri (page 166) – a round, flat unleavened bread, thicker than a roti, that is cooked on a flat pan with a little oil – and Mango Pickle (page 46). You can use either fresh or frozen cluster beans, which can be found at Indian food markets.

Serves 4
Prep time: 5 minutes
Cook time: 25 minutes

450g/1lb cluster beans (gawar) or steamed French beans

3 tbsp oil

1 tsp ajwain (carom) seeds

pinch of asafoetida

5 garlic cloves, crushed

1½ tbsp sesame seeds

¾ tsp ground turmeric

1½ tsp chilli powder

1½ tsp Coriander-cumin Powder (page 29)

¾ tsp sugar

salt, to taste

To serve
Bhakhri (page 166)

Mango Pickle (page 46)

Trim the tops of the beans.

If using cluster beans, add the beans along with 700ml/24fl oz/3 cups of water to a pressure cooker. Secure the lid and cook under full pressure for 20–25 minutes. Allow the pressure cooker to decompress before safely removing the lid. Drain the beans.

Heat the oil in a wok. Add the ajwain seeds and once they begin to crackle, add the asafoetida and the garlic. Cook until the garlic lightly caramelizes. Add the sesame seeds, drained cluster beans or steamed French beans, ground turmeric, chilli powder and coriander-cumin powder. Mix well and pour in 60ml/2fl oz/¼ cup water. Turn the heat to low and leave to cook over a low heat for 2 minutes before adding the sugar and removing the wok from the heat.

Season with salt and serve with bhakhri and mango pickle.

Note: If not using a pressure cooker, bring 1.4 litres/48fl oz/6 cups water to the boil in a deep saucepan. Add the beans and cook, partially covered, over a medium heat for 30–40 minutes. The beans should be soft but not mushy – they should retain a light crunch. Drain the beans and follow the recipe as above.

PAPADUM CURRY WITH FENUGREEK SPROUTS

METHI PAPAD

GF   DF   VG

Serves 2

Prep time: 5 minutes +
2–4 hours soaking

Cook time: 35 minutes

Research has shown numerous health benefits of consuming fenugreek, including improved brain function, lowering of cholesterol levels and reduced blood sugar. This highly nutritious seed can be found in most health stores, while the papadums (also known as lentil wafers) are widely available at Indian stores.

35g/1¼oz/¼ cup fenugreek sprouts or 3 tbsp fenugreek seeds

2 tbsp oil

¾ tsp mustard seeds

¼ tsp asafoetida

2 dried red chillies

¾ tsp chilli powder

¼ tsp ground turmeric

1 tsp Coriander-cumin Powder (page 29)

4 large papadums, broken into smaller pieces

1 tbsp grated jaggery (gur) or sugar

½ tsp Tamarind Purée (page 36)

salt, to taste

coriander (cilantro), to garnish

Parathas (page 174) or chapatis, to serve

If using fenugreek sprouts, there's no need to cook ahead, as they are tender and soft.

If using fenugreek seeds, soak the seeds in 240ml/8fl oz/1 cup water for 2–4 hours. Drain, put the soaked seeds in a pressure cooker and cover with fresh water. Secure the lid and cook under full pressure for 20 minutes. Allow the pressure cooker to decompress before safely removing the lid. Drain and set aside.

Heat the oil in a large pan over a medium heat and add the mustard seeds. Once they begin to crackle, add the asafoetida and the dried chillies. Reduce the heat to low and add the chilli powder, ground turmeric and coriander-cumin powder. Pour in 350ml/12fl oz/1½ cups water and cook for 2 minutes over a medium heat. Add the fenugreek sprouts, or cooked and drained seeds, and cook for 10–12 minutes. Add the papadums, jaggery and tamarind purée and cook for 2 minutes. Season with salt, as needed.

Garnish with coriander and serve immediately with parathas or chapatis.

Note: If not using a pressure cooker, soak the seeds in 240ml/8fl oz/ 1 cup hot water for 2 hours. Bring 480ml/16fl oz/2 cups fresh water to the boil in a saucepan. Add the seeds and their soaking water and simmer, partially covered, for 15 minutes until tender. The seeds should be soft but not mushy. Drain and follow the recipe as above.

GUAVA IN GRAVY

GF DF VG

Serves 4
Prep time: 5 minutes
Cook time: 50 minutes

I tried this dish at my sister's house after her mother-in-law prepared it. I was sceptical at first and thought it rather unusual for a fruit to be featured in a curry. However, I was soon converted after seeing the beautiful pink colour and tasting the exotic, fresh flavours! You can enjoy this dish all year round, as frozen guavas are available as wedges in Indian supermarkets.

3 tbsp oil

¾ tsp mustard seeds

½ tsp cumin seeds

½ tsp ground turmeric

2 tsp chilli powder

480ml/16fl oz/2 cups water

4 ripe guavas, seeds removed and cut into wedges, thawed if frozen

salt, to taste

2 tsp Coriander-cumin Powder (page 29)

1 tbsp grated jaggery (gur)

Roti (page 168), to serve

Heat the oil in a medium frying pan or skillet over a medium heat and add the mustard seeds. Once they begin to crackle, add the cumin seeds. Once they begin to crackle, add the ground turmeric and chilli powder along with the water. Bring to the boil and add the guava wedges, salt to taste, and the coriander-cumin powder. Cook, covered, over a low heat for 45–50 minutes until the guava is tender. Lastly, stir in the jaggery.

Serve with roti.

BUTTER BEANS IN JAGGERY AND TAMARIND
RANGOONI VAAL

▶ GF ▶ DF ▶ VG

Serves 2–4
Prep time: 5 minutes +
2–4 hours soaking
Cook time: 30 minutes

Rangooni vaal is a traditional Guajarati dish most often served at weddings. I have many fond memories of sharing this meal with loved ones on their special day. With its combination of sweet and sour, and the added benefit of being high in protein and iron, it's likely to leave a lasting impression on your guests too.

170g/6oz/1 cup dried baby butter beans (lima beans)

2½ tbsp oil

½ tsp ajwain (carom) seeds

1 tbsp finely chopped garlic

2–3 dried red chillies

pinch of asafoetida

1½ tbsp grated jaggery (gur) or brown sugar

2 tsp Tamarind Purée (page 36)

1½ tsp chilli powder

½ tsp ground turmeric

1 tsp Coriander-cumin Powder (page 29)

salt, to taste

10g/⅓oz/¼ cup chopped coriander (cilantro), to garnish

chapatis, to serve

Soak the beans in 480ml/16fl oz/2 cups hot water for 2–4 hours. Place the beans and their soaking water in a pressure cooker along with an additional 700ml/24fl oz/3 cups of fresh water. Secure the lid and cook under full pressure for 20 minutes. Allow the pressure cooker to decompress before safely removing the lid. Set aside.

Heat the oil in a large pan and add the ajwain seeds, garlic, dried chillies and asafoetida. Cook over a medium heat until the garlic starts to caramelize. Pour in the cooked beans and the water from the pressure cooker along with the jaggery, tamarind purée, chilli powder, ground turmeric, coriander-cumin powder and salt. Cook over a low heat for 6–7 minutes, adjusting the consistency with more water if necessary.

Garnish with the chopped coriander and serve with chapatis.

Note: If not using a pressure cooker, soak the beans in 480ml/16fl oz/ 2 cups hot water overnight. Bring 2 litres/64fl oz/8 cups fresh water to the boil in a saucepan. Add the beans and their soaking water and simmer, partially covered, for 2 hours until tender. Add more water if necessary. The beans should be soft and slightly mushy.

SIMPLE BUTTER PANEER

GF Q

Serves 4
Prep time: 10 minutes +
5 minutes soaking
Cook time: 10 minutes

60g/2oz/¼ cup butter

120g/4¼oz/1 cup diced paneer

60g/2oz/½ cup Cashew Paste
(page 35)

425g/16oz/2 cups Tomato Purée
(page 36)

½ tsp garam masala

¾ tsp chilli powder

½ tsp paprika

1 tsp sugar

3 tbsp double (heavy) cream

salt, to taste

To garnish (optional)
1 tbsp shredded ginger

5 slices red chilli

Roti (page 168) or rice, to serve

After years of experimenting, I have finally perfected my version of this dish. It is an easy curry for the inexperienced cook, and I have taught this recipe to my children and their friends. The feedback I get is that it is not only better than the butter paneer found in restaurants, but healthier too.

Melt 1 tablespoon of the butter in a medium non-stick pan and add the paneer cubes. Cook for 3–5 minutes on a medium-low heat, stirring continuously. Once light golden in colour, remove and set aside in a small bowl.

Add the remaining butter to the same pan and add the cashew paste. Cook until the paste thickens, then add the tomato purée, garam masala, chilli powder and paprika and cook for 5–7 minutes. Stir well, return the paneer to the pan along with 240ml/8fl oz/1 cup water. Cook over a medium heat until the mixture thickens and the oil rises to the surface. Add the sugar and cream, stir well to combine and warm through for another 5 minutes.

Season the mixture with salt and garnish with ginger and chillies, if using. Serve warm with roti or rice.

PAV BHAJI

Serves 4

Prep time: 20 minutes +
2 hours soaking

Cook time: 40–45 minutes

For the green peas

85g/3oz/½ cup dried whole green
peas or yellow peas, rinsed

480ml/16fl oz/2 cups hot water

For the pav bhaji

60g/2oz/½ cup chopped green
bell pepper

125ml/4fl oz/½ cup water

320g/11¼oz/2 cups chopped ripe
Roma tomatoes

2 potatoes, boiled, peeled and
roughly chopped

2½ tsp Kashmiri chilli powder

2 tbsp Garlic Paste (page 31)

170g/6oz/¾ cup butter, preferably
Amul

2½ tbsp Mumbai bhaji pav
masala (available at Indian
supermarkets)

salt, to taste

30g/1oz/¾ cup finely chopped
coriander (cilantro)

60g/2oz/½ cup finely chopped
red onion

1 tsp fresh lime juice

Bombay pav bhaji is quintessential Mumbai street food and I simply could not omit it from this recipe book. Pav (bread) and bhaji (mixed vegetables) make up this smooth, savoury and spicy dish. Interestingly, it was created when the workers at textile mills were getting less and less time to eat and heavy meals consumed at lunchtime resulted in a lack of energy later in the afternoon. Curry and roti were thus replaced with bread and vegetables and this iconic dish was born.

Tracking down an authentic recipe was painstaking! After moving to the States, I ate pav bhaji on numerous occasions and each time it was different. I soon realized that every Indian household has their own preferred method. I am confident that this recipe is as close as you will get to the real thing. If you can, source Amul butter, a brand of unsalted butter available at Indian supermarkets. If you are cutting down on fat, you can still get great results with halving the amount of butter used here.

Soak the dried peas in the water in a pressure cooker for 2 hours. Secure the lid and cook under full pressure for 25 minutes. Lower the heat and simmer for another 10 minutes. Allow the pressure cooker to decompress before safely removing the lid. Allow to cool then mash until smooth. Set aside.

Heat a large frying pan or skillet over a medium heat and add the chopped bell peppers. Add half the water and cook until the peppers soften. Add the chopped tomatoes and cook for 2 minutes. Add the cooked and chopped potatoes, mashing them into the pan using a potato masher. Add 75g/2¾oz/½ cup of the cooked green peas, 1½ teaspoons of the chilli powder and 1½ tablespoons of the garlic paste. Add 60g/2oz/¼ cup of the butter and continue to mix and stir, ensuring the vegetables do not stick to the pan. Mash the vegetables, adding the remaining water, and mix well. Add another 60g/2oz/¼ cup of the butter, followed by 1½ tablespoons of the Mumbai bhaji masala, salt and 20g/¾oz/½ cup of the finely chopped coriander. Continue to mix and mash until the mixture has thickened and the oil has separated.

PAV BHAJI (CONTINUED)

For the toasted bread rolls

60g/2oz/¼ cup butter

40g/1½oz/1 cup finely chopped coriander (cilantro)

pinch of chilli powder

1 tsp Mumbai bhaji pav masala

4 soft white bread rolls, sliced in half

Use a spatula to push the pav bhaji to the sides of the pan and add the remaining butter to the centre of the pan. Add the onions to the melted butter, the remaining ½ tablespoon garlic paste, 1 teaspoon chilli powder, 1 tablespoon Mumbai bhaji masala and the remaining chopped coriander. Mix well and cook for 3–5 minutes. Add the lime juice. Fold the cooked vegetables from the sides of the pan into the onion mixture and continue to cook and mash the bhaji to a purée. Add another 60ml/2fl oz/¼ cup water if needed. Set aside and keep warm.

For the toasted bread rolls, heat the butter in a large frying pan or skillet and add the coriander, chilli powder, and Mumbai bhaji masala. Spread the mixture out in the pan and once the butter has completely melted, spread all 8 halves of the sliced buns onto the pan, covering the mixture, toasting lightly on both sides for 10–15 seconds, absorbing the flavours.

To serve

1 tbsp finely chopped coriander (cilantro)

60g/2oz/½ cup finely chopped red onion

1 lime, cut into 4 wedges

4 tsp butter

To serve, divide the bhaji between 4 bowls or plates and top with chopped coriander. Add the onions, toasted bread rolls, lime wedges for squeezing and a teaspoon of butter to each serving.

Note: If not using a pressure cooker, place the rinsed peas in a deep saucepan and cover with 1.9 litres/64fl oz/8 cups hot water. Leave to soak for 2 hours. Bring the peas and soaking water to the boil, then partially cover with a lid and cook over a medium heat for 1½ hours until the peas are mushy.

Note: Leftover green peas can be stored in a zip-top bag in the freezer for 3 months. Thaw before using.

TARO AND RIDGE GOURD CURRY

TURIA PAATRA NU SHAAK

GF · DF · VG

Serves 4
Prep time: 10 minutes
Cook time: 30–35 minutes

2 tbsp oil

½ tsp ajwain (carom) seeds

2 garlic cloves, sliced

pinch of asafoetida

¼ tsp ground turmeric

115g/4oz/1 cup diced ridge gourd
(turia), or courgette (zucchini)

1 tsp Coriander-cumin Powder
(page 29)

½ tsp Garlic Paste (page 31)

½ tsp Ginger Paste (page 32)

½ tsp garam masala

¼ tsp bicarbonate of soda
(baking soda)

salt, to taste

2 rolls unseasoned and steamed
Layered Taro Leaves (page 100),
or use store-bought frozen and
thawed patras, sliced

1 tsp sugar

1 tsp fresh lime juice

To garnish
1 tbsp chopped coriander
(cilantro)

small garlic cloves (optional)

chapatis, to serve

This traditional Gujarati dish, often served at weddings, is
high in protein and packed with vegetables, making it tasty and
healthy. It is also sweet and spicy, leaving a pleasant taste in the
mouth. I have been serving this at Diwali parties for years now
and it is very well-received (a friend even called me after the
party enquiring about any leftovers!). Thanks to my *maasi*
(my mother's sister) for sharing her recipe.

Ridge gourd, also known as luffa or turai, is a popular Indian
vegetable. It is long, ridged and tapers at one end. The hard,
dark-green skin is generally peeled off. You can use courgette
(zucchini) if ridge gourd isn't available.

If you are reducing calories, this dish is a good option as taro
is filling, with more fibre and fewer calories than its cousin the
potato. If you don't have time to make your own layered taro
leaves, store-bought frozen patras work just as well.

Heat the oil in a frying pan or skillet over a medium heat and add the
ajwain seeds. Once they begin to crackle, add the garlic, asafoetida and
ground turmeric and cook for 2–3 minutes. Add the ridge gourd along
with 480ml/16fl oz/2 cups water. Mix well then add the coriander-cumin
powder, garlic and ginger pastes, garam masala, bicarbonate of soda and
salt. Cover the pan and cook over a medium-low heat for 18–20 minutes
until the ridge gourd becomes tender. Add another 125ml/4fl oz/½ cup
water along with the taro slices and simmer for 10–12 minutes.

Remove the pan from the heat and gently stir in the sugar and lime
juice, being careful not to break up the taro. Add a little more water
if the curry is dry. Garnish with the coriander and the garlic cloves,
if using.

Serve with chapatis.

SURTI UNDHIYU

UBADIYU

DF   VG

Serves 6
Prep time: 15 minutes
Cook time: 50 minutes

Fresh and varied winter vegetables bring a colourful exuberance to vegetable markets Gujarat. Leafy greens rub shoulders with root veg, a plethora of beans and the loveliest small round aubergines (eggplants) – brinjals! Undhiyu is a typical winter mixed-vegetable dish and each home has its own masala that goes into its tempering mix.

For the pan-fried vegetables
480ml/16fl oz/2 cups oil

6–8 baby aubergines (eggplants), stems removed and a deep criss-cross incision made in each aubergine (so it's quartered but not all the way)

8–10 baby potatoes, peeled

1 sweet potato, peeled and cut into 1cm (½-inch) thick slices

250g/9oz frozen or fresh purple yam (ratalu), thawed if frozen, cut into 2.5cm (1-inch) dice

1 unripe banana, cut into 1cm (½-inch) thick slices

For the undhiyu paste
45g/1½oz/⅓ cup peanuts

25g/1oz/¼ cup chopped garlic scapes (optional)

6cm (2½-inch) piece of fresh ginger, peeled

6–7 garlic cloves

5–6 green chillies, stems removed

½ tsp ground turmeric

¼ tsp asafoetida

3 tbsp sugar

1½ tsp lime juice

1½ tsp salt

40g/1½oz/1 cup finely chopped coriander (cilantro)

For the green vegetables
350g/12oz fresh or frozen pigeon peas (tuver lilva)

240ml/8fl oz/1 cup groundnut (peanut) oil

1 tsp ajwain (carom) seeds

½ tsp asafoetida

350g/12oz fresh or frozen surti papdi, or runner beans, ends trimmed and string removed if fresh

175g/6oz fresh or frozen surti lilva or frozen butter (Lima) beans

½ tsp bicarbonate of soda (baking soda)

1 tsp salt

700ml/24fl oz/3 cups warm water

1 quantity Fenugreek Dumplings (page 144)

To finish
10g/⅓oz/¼ cup chopped coriander (cilantro)

25g/1oz/¼ cup chopped garlic scapes (optional)

Pooris (page 167) or Roti (page 168), to serve

Heat the oil for the pan-fried vegetables in a frying pan or skillet over a medium heat. Add the aubergines and fry for 6–7 minutes, then transfer to a plate. Add the potatoes, sweet potato and purple yam to the pan and fry for 6 minutes, then transfer to another plate. Repeat with the banana slices, again cooking for 6 minutes, and transfer to a third plate.

To make the undhiyu paste, combine all the ingredients except for the coriander in a blender or food processor and blend to a paste. Stir in the chopped coriander and set aside while you cook the green vegetables.

Put half the pigeon peas in a food processor and crush for 8–10 seconds, then set aside. Heat the oil in a heavy-bottomed saucepan over a medium heat, add the ajwain seeds and cook until they begin to crackle. Add the asafoetida and cook for 3–4 seconds, until fragrant. Add the surti papdi, surti lilva and bicarbonate of soda and cook for 6–8 minutes. Add the whole and crushed pigeon peas and cook for another 6–8 minutes, until the vegetables are cooked through. Add the salt and prepared undhiyu paste and cook for another 8–10 minutes (the paste should be separated from the oil). Add the warm water and bring to the boil for 2–3 minutes.

Next add the pan-fried potato, sweet potato and yam and gently mix. Taste for salt, then arrange the aubergines, bananas and fenugreek dumplings on top. Do not stir after this point, as the vegetables and dumplings can break easily. Cover the pan with a lid and cook over a low heat for 15–18 minutes. It should have the consistency of a sauce, so add another 125ml/4fl oz/½ cup water, if needed, to thin it out.

Garnish with the chopped coriander and garlic scapes, if using. Serve hot with pooris or roti.

BREADS

BHAKHRI

DF   VG

This is one of my favourite types of bread because it is so versatile. It can stand up to any curry, but it goes particularly well with green vegetable dishes such as the Surti Lilva (page 140). It makes a reliable everyday dinner bread, but I also enjoy it warm for breakfast.

The dough can be refrigerated for up to 3 days, meaning, if you're anything like me, you can have freshly made bhakhri every night (or morning) of the week.

Serves 4
Prep time: 10 minutes +
15 minutes resting
Cook time: 35 minutes

200g/7oz/1½ cups wholemeal (wholewheat) flour

3 tbsp oil, plus extra for brushing

7 tbsp warm water

Mango Pickle (page 46), to serve

Combine the flour and oil in a mixing bowl and mix it well. Add the warm water and knead for 3–5 minutes to make a stiff and smooth dough, adding another teaspoon of water if needed. Cover the bowl with a plate or tea (dish) towel and set aside to rest for 15 minutes.

Divide the dough into 8 equal portions and roll into balls. Preheat a flat griddle or a non-stick frying pan or skillet over a medium heat. Flatten each ball into a 13cm (5-inch) disc. Place the disc on the griddle and cook for 1–2 minutes until light brown spots appear on the underside. Turn over and cook for another minute. Brush 1 teaspoon oil over the bhakhri, then flip it again to fry for 30 seconds. Flip again and cook for another 30 seconds. Transfer to a plate and repeat with the remaining dough.

Serve with mango pickle.

POORI

DF   VG   Q

Serves 4
Prep time: 10 minutes +
15 minutes resting
Cook time: 5 minutes

200g/7oz/1½ cups wholemeal
   (wholewheat) flour

3 tbsp oil, plus 700ml/24fl oz/
   3 cups for deep-frying, and
   extra for rubbing

7 tbsp warm water

Poori is a puffed deep-fried bread, normally prepared for guests and on special occasions. It is so much fun to make fresh pooris and serve them hot to the guests.

In Gujarati culture, fried foods are often regarded as a sign of a good living. These days people have become very health conscious but in ancient times, you were often judged by your guests depending on how rich and buttery your food was. Roti and rotlo (millet bread) are still more commonly served as everyday food and it would be impolite to serve them to guests. In fact, guests may feel less valued or insulted if you serve them anything other than deep-fried bread.

In a large bowl, combine the flour and the 3 tablespoons of oil. Mix well. Add the warm water and mix together. Knead in the bowl for 3–4 minutes. Rub a teaspoon of oil in your hands to smooth the dough and knead for another 2 minutes until it is smooth and tight. Cover the bowl with a plate or tea (dish) towel and set aside to rest for 15 minutes.

Divide the dough into 16 equal portions and roll out each piece to a disc, about 7.5cm (3 inches) in diameter.

Heat the oil for deep-frying in a deep saucepan over a medium heat. Add 2–3 pooris, to avoid overcrowding, and fry for 3–4 seconds, until lightly golden and puffed. Turn and fry for another 3–4 seconds, or until lightly golden. Using a slotted spoon or skimmer, transfer the pooris to a paper towel-lined plate to drain. Repeat with the remaining pooris.

ROTI

ROTLI

What I love best about rotli (Gujarati for roti) is that it is prepared and brought to the table one at a time. My older brother would insist on serving me first, even when I was an adult, freshly made rotli with melted ghee on top. Whenever I eat or make a fresh rotli, I am reminded of his kindness and generosity and the many meals he and my sister-in-law prepared for me whenever I visited India. You will be dearly missed, dear brother.

Serves 6
Prep time: 15 minutes +
15 minutes resting
Cook time: 5–10 minutes

For the roti
200g/7oz/1½ cups wholemeal (wholewheat) flour, or see Note below, plus 70g/2½oz/½ cup for dusting

2 tsp oil

125ml/4fl oz/½ cup warm water

To serve
4 tbsp ghee

Place the flour(s) in a bowl and make a well in the centre. Pour in 1 teaspoon of the oil and mix well. Slowly add 60ml/2fl oz/¼ cup of the warm water and mix well. Gradually add the remaining water until a dough forms. Add 1–2 teaspoons more water if needed.

Coat the dough with the remaining teaspoon of oil and knead for 2–3 minutes until it is soft, smooth and elastic. Cover the bowl with an airtight lid and set aside for 15 minutes. Knead the dough one last time before dividing into 12 equal-sized portions. Roll each portion into a ball and flatten using the palm of your hand. Place the balls of dough onto a lightly floured work surface and roll each one into a thin circle, approximately 13cm (5 inches) in diameter, continually dusting with flour to prevent sticking. The circles should be even in thickness.

Heat a flat frying pan or skillet over a medium-high heat and, once hot, place a disc of rolled dough directly onto the pan. Cook for 8–10 seconds, then flip over and cook the other side for the same length of time. To puff it up, preheat a gas stove over a high heat and, using tongs, place the rotli directly onto the flame for 2 seconds on each side until puffed. (Alternatively, place a heatproof rack on a stove top and add the rotli.) Immediately spread 1 tsp of ghee onto the rotli and set aside. Cook the rest of the rotli.

Note: Making a multigrain roti is just as easy. Simply replace the wholemeal flour with the following combination and follow the method:
• 65g/2½oz/½ cup wholemeal (wholewheat) flour, plus extra for dusting
• 30g/1oz/¼ cup quinoa or sorghum (jowar) flour
• 30g/1oz/¼ cup millet (bajra) flour
• 25g/1oz/¼ cup soya (soy) flour
• 30g/1oz/¼ cup black lentil (urad) flour

SWEET LENTIL BREAD
PURAN POLI OR VEDMI

This sweet bread brings back one particular memory when I celebrated Diwali with 100 extended family members. Bringing nothing but positive energies and togetherness, this special-occasion dish is normally eaten with kadhi (Spiced Yogurt Soup, page 125) on the day of Diwali. It is also part of the biggest festival and holds a very special place in a Gujarati thali (see page 106).

This type of bread always has a sweet and fragrant, spiced filling (puran) made with smooth pigeon pea (toor) dal or chickpea dal.

Serves 4
Prep time: 30 minutes
Cook time: 1 hour 10 minutes

180g/6¼oz/1 cup dried split pigeon peas (toor dal)

700ml/24fl oz/3 cups water

60g/2oz/¼ cup plus 2 tsp sugar

½ tsp ground cardamom

¼ tsp ground nutmeg

1 tsp white poppy seeds

1 quantity wholemeal (wholewheat) Roti dough (see opposite)

60g/2oz/½ cup plain (all-purpose) flour, for dusting

3 tbsp ghee, to serve

Wash the pigeon peas under cold, running water until the water runs clear. Place the rinsed pigeon peas in a pressure cooker along with the water. Secure the lid and cook under full pressure for 30 minutes. Allow the pressure cooker to decompress before safely removing the lid.

Transfer the cooked pigeon peas to a medium saucepan, add the sugar and stir continuously for 15 minutes over a medium heat, until the mixture thickens. Remove from the heat and set aside to cool. Add the cardamom, nutmeg and poppy seeds and mix well. Divide the mixture into 8 equal portions.

Roll the dough into circles, about 7.5cm (3 inches) in diameter and 5mm (¼-inch) thick. Place a portion of the filling in the centre and bring the edges of the dough up over the filling. Pinch the edges together and seal the filling. Dust the dough and carefully roll the filled dough to a 10cm (4-inch) disc.

Heat a dry frying pan or skillet over a medium heat. Place the bread in the pan and cook for 45 seconds on one side, flip over and cook for 30 seconds on the second side, or until golden. Repeat with the remaining breads. Brush 1 tsp ghee on top of each and serve hot.

Note: If not using a pressure cooker, place the rinsed peas in a deep saucepan and cover with 2 litres/64fl oz/8 cups hot water. Leave to soak for 4 hours. Bring the peas and soaking water to the boil, skimming off froth as needed. Cover and cook over a medium heat for 1½ hours until the peas are very mushy.

DOUBLE-LAYERED ROTI
PAD WALI ROTLI

This recipe is really unique because you make two roti at the same time, reducing the preparation time by half. I simply love it!

Pad wali rotli always remind me of the mango season in India (April–July) and the long summer breaks, which end just before the monsoon season starts. Nothing beats the bright, ripe flesh of a sweet mango and we use it to make fresh mango pulp (keri no ras) to serve alongside double-layered roti.

Serves 6
Prep time: 15 minutes +
15 minutes resting
Cook time: 15 minutes

200g/7oz/1½ cups wholemeal (wholewheat) flour, plus 70g/2½oz/½ cup for dusting

2 tsp oil, plus extra for dipping

125ml/4fl oz/½ cup warm water

To serve
4 tbsp ghee

mango pulp (optional)

Place the flour in a bowl and make a well in the centre. Pour in 1 teaspoon of the oil and mix well. Slowly add 60ml/2fl oz/¼ cup of the warm water and mix again. Gradually add the remaining water until a dough forms. Add 1–2 teaspoons more water if needed.

Coat the dough with the remaining teaspoon of oil and knead for 2–3 minutes until it is soft, smooth and elastic. Cover the bowl with an airtight lid and set aside for 15 minutes. Knead the dough one last time before dividing into 12 equal-sized portions. Shape each one into a smooth ball.

Prepare two small bowls, one with oil for dipping and the other with flour. Take a dough ball in each hand, dip both balls slightly in oil to coat one side, then dip the oiled sides into the flour. Press the two balls together, with the floured sides in contact.

Generously dust the dough ball with flour, then roll it out into a 13–15cm (5–6-inch) disc. (Add more flour if necessary.) Do not apply too much pressure – there should be two visible layers. Repeat with the remaining dough balls, to make 6 discs in total, and keep the discs covered as you cook each one.

Heat a non-stick frying pan or skillet over a medium heat. Add a roti and cook for 20–30 seconds, until light brown spots appear on the underside. Turn and cook for another 30 seconds, until cooked through. Remove from the heat and gently tap the roti to separate the layers.

Brush 1 tsp ghee over each hot roti and serve immediately with mango pulp, if using. Repeat the process with the remaining 5 discs.

DHEBRA

BAJRA NA THEPLA

My father-in-law loves my dhebras and asks for them whenever he visits me. On the last occasion, he would sneak one every morning so that he didn't have to share them! He is such a fan that I often have couriered a fresh batch of dhebras to him across the country. I can just imagine his delight when he opened the overnight parcel.

Serves 4
Prep time: 15 minutes +
10 minutes resting
Cook time: 25 minutes

130g/4½oz/1 cup wholemeal (wholewheat) flour

40g/1½oz/⅓ cup millet (bajra) flour

½ tsp ground turmeric

1 tbsp plus 1 tsp Green Chilli Paste (page 32)

1½ tbsp sesame seeds, plus extra to serve

¾ tsp ajwain (carom) seeds

1 tbsp brown sugar

1 tsp salt, or to taste

1½ tsp Ginger Paste (page 32)

4 tbsp ghee or oil, plus extra oil for cooking

70g/2½oz/⅓ cup plain full-fat yogurt or Strained Yogurt (page 37)

40g/1½oz/1½ cups fresh chopped fenugreek leaves (methi), washed and patted dry, or use finely chopped spinach leaves

Mango Pickle (page 46) or Masala Chai (page 188), to serve

Combine the flours, ground turmeric, green chilli paste, sesame seeds, ajwain seeds, sugar, salt and ginger paste in a large bowl. Add the ghee and yogurt and mix well. Add the chopped fenugreek leaves and mix again. Knead the dough for 6–8 minutes until smooth, then cover the bowl tightly with a lid and set aside for 10 minutes.

Knead a second time and divide the mixture into 8 equal-sized portions. Roll each portion into a ball, then flatten slightly.

Roll each flattened ball of dough between two sheets of parchment paper into discs 13cm (5 inches) in diameter, ensuring they are of even thickness.

Heat a large frying pan or skillet over a medium heat. Once hot, add 1 teaspoon of oil to grease the pan. Then place a disc of dough in the pan. Cook for 1½–2 minutes, pressing down gently with a spatula, until the underside has light brown spots. Flip, then drizzle ½ teaspoon of oil on top of the dhebra. Flip again, add another ½ teaspoon of oil, and cook for 1 minute. Remove from the pan and place on a plate. Repeat the procedure for the remaining dhebras.

Sprinkle with sesame seeds and serve with mango pickle or masala chai.

TAPIOCA PARATHA

SABUDANA THALIPEETH

GF   DF   VG

Several years ago, in the midst of all the major Indian festivals, my husband and I took a trip to a Hindu temple in the Bay Area of California. We felt a renewed sense of happiness and promise (the way good news from a doctor can bring) and celebrated the day by nipping behind the temple at lunchtime to visit a small Indian restaurant. We saw sabudana thalipeeth on the menu and ordered it. It was so good, albeit a rather unusual dish for me. I immediately fell in love with it and the fact that it went so well with pickle. I have made it several times since then, serving it alongside tomato chutney and homemade pickles.

Serves 6
Prep time: 10 minutes +
overnight soaking
Cook time: 30 minutes

150g/5½oz/1 cup sago (sabudana or tapioca pearls)

240ml/8fl oz/1 cup water

2 potatoes, boiled, peeled and mashed

2 tbsp roasted peanuts, crushed

2 tbsp chopped coriander (cilantro)

2 tbsp finely chopped green chillies

2 tsp fresh lemon juice

1 tsp Ginger Paste (page 32)

½ tsp cumin seeds, slightly crushed

salt, to taste

oil, for frying

Mango Pickle (page 46) or Peanut Chutney (page 43), to serve

Place the sago in a bowl with the water. Cover and leave to soak overnight (or minimum 2 hours). Drain well and transfer to a large bowl along with the remaining ingredients apart from the oil. Mix well.

Knead the mixture for 2–3 minutes until smooth. Divide the mixture into 6 equal-sized portions and roll each portion into a ball. Flatten the balls using the palm of your hands and shape into discs.

Roll each disc between two sheets of parchment paper to 13–15cm (5–6-inches) in diameter, ensuring they are of even thickness.

Heat a frying pan or skillet over a medium heat. Once hot, heat 1 teaspoon of oil in the pan and place one paratha disc in the pan. Cook for 2½ minutes, then turn. Sprinkle with ½ teaspoon of oil and cook for 2 minutes. Flip again, and add another ½ teaspoon of oil. Remove from the pan and repeat the procedure for the remaining parathas.

Serve hot with mango pickle or peanut chutney.

CLASSIC GUJARATI: THE BREADS

All Gujarati meals include freshly made bread of one sort or another. Bread is a tool as well as a food, rolled or broken and used to dip into sauces, soak up spices, stuff with vegetables or smear with chutney or ghee. The original Indian breads are flat, meaning unleavened, and while wheat flour is used for most breads, the way the dough is kneaded with the right amounts of oil and water is what distinguishes the flavours and textures of one bread from another.

Roti (page 168), known as rotli in Gujarati, is made daily in most homes across India, mostly eaten at lunch. This flatbread is generally rolled out into thin 13cm (5-inch) discs and, as the name suggests, roasted on both sides on a hot griddle or skillet where it puffs up like a balloon. For Gujaratis, there should not be a single brown spot on its cream-coloured surface! The rotli is then generously patted all over with ghee – preferably traditional full-fat ghee known as desi – so that it remains soft even a couple of hours later.

Bhakhri (page 166), also known as crispy chapati, is made from a tightly kneaded, almost crumbly dough, using lots of oil and less water than roti. It too is rolled out to a 13cm (5-inch) disc but it is double the thickness of roti. Whereas roti are eaten at lunch, bhakhri tend to be served with the lighter meal at dinner.

Pooris (page 167) are prepared for festive occasions, especially when more people are sharing a meal, and usually accompany a thali (page 106). Pooris are rolled into discs, about 7.5cm (3 inches) across, and deep-fried so that they puff up. Gujjus serve pooris alongside sweet or savoury dishes: poori-shrikhand, poori-bhaji (curried or dry potato vegetable) and ras-poori (mango purée) are some of the well-loved combinations.

Rotlo (plural rotla) also known as millet bread, is made with millet flour (bajra), sorghum flour (jowar), or in certain areas, white maize (makai no rotlo). In urban areas, rotla tend to be eaten in the winter months but in rural and tribal areas they are the staple throughout the year. Unlike other flatbreads in Gujarat, rotla are not rolled out; instead the ball of dough is patted between the palms moistened with water to fashion a disc, the damp palms easing the movement of the dough. Rotla are roasted on clay skillets, and a well-made rotlo will puff up, its thinner crust rising such that it can be split open like a pocket and smeared inside with ghee.

One bread you won't find in Gujarat households is naan. This is a leavened bread made using yeast, yogurt or buttermilk, introduced to the sub-continent by Muslims originating from central Asia.

PEARL MILLET BREAD
BAJRA NA ROTLO

Q

Traditionally this rotlo is cooked in an earthen skillet, which is a common piece of cookware in Gujarati households. And if you have one, go ahead and use it! But if not, a cast-iron frying pan or skillet works just as well for all practical purposes.

Serves 4
Prep time: 15 minutes
Cook time: 20 minutes

¼ tsp salt

125ml/4fl oz/½ cup water

120g/4¼oz/1 cup millet (bajra) flour, plus extra for dusting

4 tsp wholemeal (wholewheat) flour, plus extra for dusting

To serve
3 tbsp ghee

3–4 tbsp grated jaggery (gur)

Dissolve the salt in the water in a small bowl.

Place the flours in a mixing bowl. Add the salty water and mix into the flour. Once combined, transfer the mixture to a floured work surface and knead for 3–4 minutes, until the dough is soft and pliable. Add a little more water if needed.

Divide the dough into 4 equal portions and shape into balls. Flour the work surface again and place a ball on top. Place a ball of dough between your palms, then pat and flatten it into a 13cm (5-inch) disc. (Alternatively, use a rolling pin to roll out the dough.)

Heat a cast-iron frying pan or skillet over a medium heat. Place a disc in the pan and cook for 2–3 minutes, then flip and cook for another 1–2 minutes, until cooked through and puffed up. Repeat with the remaining dough.

Transfer the rotlo to a plate and spread 2 tsp ghee over it. Serve hot with a side of jaggery.

RICE & KHICHDI

CRACKED WHEAT KHICHDI
THULI

DF   VG

My thuli (cracked wheat and yellow mung/moong dal) is simmered in a gentle combination of cumin and ginger, delivering a tasty, complete meal. Rich in iron and high in fibre, I love it with cracked wheat although many people use rice in place of cracked wheat. I think kadhi, Spiced Yogurt Soup (page 125) is a great accompaniment, but overall it needs little else to accompany it. It's a versatile dish which can be enjoyed with milk for an excellent, nutritious breakfast.

This recipe was handed down to me by my beloved grandmother. Her healthy outlook on life is evident in the 101 years she spent with us. Her values were simple: healthy, homemade meals made with love. She is affectionately remembered every time I make thuli – and now I can share it with you, ensuring her legacy lives on.

Serves 4
Prep time: 5 minutes +
1 hour soaking
Cook time: 25 minutes

50g/1¾oz/¼ cup split mung beans (mung/moong dal) or split red lentils (masoor dal)

85g/3oz/½ cup uncooked cracked (bulgur) wheat

800ml/28fl oz/3½ cups water

1½ tbsp ghee, plus 1 tsp to serve

1 tsp cumin seeds

2 tsp minced ginger

1 tsp salt, or to taste

milk or Spiced Yogurt Soup (page 125), to serve (optional)

Rinse the mung dal and cracked wheat under running water until the water runs clear. Place in a bowl along with 240ml/8fl oz/1 cup of the measured water and leave to soak for 1 hour. Drain well, discard the soaking water and set aside.

Heat the ghee in a medium saucepan and, once hot, add the cumin seeds. When the seeds begin to crackle, add the ginger, salt and remaining water. Bring to the boil and add the soaked grains. Partially cover the pan with a lid and cook over a medium heat for 10 minutes, then turn the heat to low and cook for a further 15 minutes.

Place a teaspoon of ghee (at room temperature) on top and serve warm with milk or spiced yogurt soup, if using.

BURNT GARLIC RICE

DF   VG   Q

Serves 4
Prep time: 10 minutes
Cook time: 10–15 minutes

3 tbsp oil

6 garlic cloves, finely chopped

250g/9oz/1 cup firm tofu, diced
   into 2.5cm (1-inch) cubes

1½ tbsp finely chopped Thai
   green chillies

3 tbsp soy sauce

1½ tbsp brown sugar

2 cups cooked jasmine rice
   (see Note)

4 tbsp roughly chopped basil

salt, to taste

My elder daughter studied in London and on one visit to her, we had an incredible rice dish that she absolutely loved. Relying on memory, I took it upon myself to replicate the dish for her to enjoy at home. The rice has a unique and crisp textural element. The key is to cook the rice until it sticks to the pan to create those deeply delicious flavours and textures. (This essential component is called socarrat in Spanish paella.) Keep your eye on the rice as it cooks – you do not want to burn the rice crust and render it bitter and unpalatable.

Heat the oil in a frying pan or skillet over a medium heat. Add the garlic and sauté for a minute, until light brown. Add the tofu and sauté for another 3–4 minutes. Stir in the green chillies.

Push the mixture to the side of the pan, then add the soy sauce and brown sugar and cook until it begins to bubble. Add the rice, mix well and fry for 3 minutes.

Stir in the basil and season with salt. Cook for another 3–4 minutes, untouched, until the rice sticks to the bottom. Transfer to a serving dish and serve warm.

Note: Leftover rice can be used for this recipe. To avoid food poisoning, it is essential that leftover rice is adequately chilled soon after it is cooked. If in doubt, cook a fresh batch before making the recipe.

TAPIOCA RED PEARLS DELIGHT
SABUDANA KHICHDI WITH BEETROOT

GF DF VG

Serves 3
Prep time: 10 minutes +
2–3 hours soaking
Cook time: 10 minutes

Traditionally, this is made with potato and cumin seeds, but my version uses beetroot and mustard seeds. I simply love the deep, earthy flavours of the beetroot and the colour is just delightful, as you can well imagine! A favourite breakfast item, sabudana khichdi is a popular fasting food (upvas) for major festivals like Navratri, Ekadashi and Shivratri. I love it with plain yogurt.

110g/3¾oz/¾ cup sago (sabudana or tapioca pearls)

300ml/10½fl oz/1¼ cups water

salt, to taste

2 tsp fresh lime juice

1½ tbsp oil

½ tsp mustard seeds

8–10 fresh curry leaves

2–3 tbsp raw or roasted peanuts

150g/5½oz/1 cup peeled and diced cooked beetroot (beet)

2–3 green chillies, stems removed and sliced

1 tsp sugar

1 tbsp chopped coriander (cilantro)

215g/7½oz/1 cup plain full-fat yogurt, to serve (optional)

Rinse the sago under cold, running water until the water runs clear. Place in a bowl with the water and cover, leaving to soak for 2–3 hours. Drain well and transfer to a medium bowl. Add the salt and lime juice and toss it well.

Heat the oil in a non-stick frying pan or skillet and add the mustard seeds. Once they begin to crackle, add the curry leaves and peanuts and cook over a low heat for 3 minutes, stirring occasionally. Add the beetroot and the green chillies and cook for another 2 minutes before adding the sago/lime mixture to the pan. Combine well and cook for 5–6 minutes until the sago becomes transparent. Stir in the sugar and remove the pan from the heat.

Transfer to a serving platter, garnish with the chopped coriander, and serve with the yogurt, if using.

Note: If you would like to try the more traditional sabudana khichdi, follow the same recipe as above, but replace the mustard seeds with ¾ teaspoon cumin seeds and use 2 peeled potatoes (diced into 2cm/¾-inch pieces) in place of the beetroot. Since the diced potatoes will be uncooked, increase the cooking time to ensure the potatoes are cooked until tender. Add the green chillies and cook for another minute before adding the sago/lime mixture to the pan. Combine well and cook until the sago becomes transparent. Stir in the sugar and remove the pan from the heat.

YELLOW RICE

KHICHDI

GF   DF   VG

This trusted and reliable dish is great to prepare on lazy days that require a tasty quick fix. We love serving this at home with pea and potato curry (Aloo Mutter in Gravy, page 134). You can buy khichdi rice in Indian supermarkets, but basmati or other rice will work perfectly well.

Serves 4
Prep time: 10 minutes +
1 hour soaking
Cook time: 45 minutes

180g/6¼oz/1 cup rice

90g/3¼oz/½ cup dried split pigeon
  peas (toor dal)

½ tsp ground turmeric

1½ tsp salt

To serve
ghee

Spiced Yogurt Soup (page 125)
  (optional)

papadums

Mango and Red Onion
  Kachumber (page 49)

Mango Pickle (page 46)

Rinse the rice and the pigeon peas and place in separate bowls with enough water to cover. Soak for 1 hour. Drain well.

Bring 1.4 litres/48fl oz/6 cups of water to the boil in a saucepan. Add the turmeric and salt, then the pigeon peas, partially cover the pan, and reduce the heat to medium. Skim any froth from the surface. Cook for 20 minutes, then add the rice with another 700ml/24fl oz/ 3 cups of water and cover again. Reduce the heat to low and cook for 18–20 minutes until the dal and rice are cooked through. Add another 60–125ml/2–4fl oz/¼–½ cup water if needed and cook for a final 3–4 minutes. Turn the heat off and leave the pan, covered, on the stove so the khichdi stays warm.

Serve warm with ghee, spiced yogurt soup, papadums, kachumber and mango pickle.

Note: If using a pressure cooker, rinse the rice and pigeon peas and place in the cooker with 800ml/28fl oz/3½ cups of water. Add the turmeric and salt and mix well. Secure the lid and let the dal and rice soak for 2 hours, then cook under full pressure for 20–25 minutes. Allow the pressure cooker to decompress before safely removing the lid.

CHUTNEY PULAO

KOTHMIRA RICE

GF   DF   VG   Q

Serves 3–4
Prep time: 5 minutes
Cook time: 30 minutes

1 tbsp corn or coconut oil

85g/3oz/¾ cup chopped onion

225g/8oz/1¼ cups basmati rice

700ml/24fl oz/3 cups
  vegetable stock

110g/3¾oz/½ cup Green Paste
  (page 30)

65g/2¼oz/½ cup frozen shelled
  edamame, petits pois or garden
  peas, thawed

10g/⅓oz/¼ cup chopped
  coriander (cilantro)

Spiced Yogurt Soup (page 125),
  to serve

Brilliant green colours always welcome you to the dinner plate. To do that, I use coriander in almost every Indian dish I prepare. In this recipe, the aromas of fresh coriander leaves, garlic and green chilli give plain old white rice a nice kick. It's different and easy to prepare. I grow my coriander in a small pot near my kitchen window. It's one of the easiest herbs to grow in a pot or your garden, even if you don't have green fingers.

Heat the oil in a frying pan or skillet over a medium heat. Add the onion and sauté for 4–5 minutes. Add the rice and sauté for 5–7 minutes, stirring gently. Pour in the stock and green paste and bring to the boil. Reduce the heat to medium-low, cover and cook for 12–15 minutes. Add the edamame, sprinkle the coriander on top, cover and cook for another 4 minutes, until cooked through.

Serve with spiced yogurt soup.

DRINKS & DESSERTS

MASALA CHAI

GF   Q

Masala chai is a big deal in India – and an even bigger deal in our house! Chai means 'Good Morning' in our family. It certainly keeps us connected, as we all share a common love for it.

India consumes 837,000 tons of chai every year and the ritual of drinking it is an integral part of the culture. Without fail, my darling husband prepares a cup for us every morning. It is something I so look forward to because the smell of the glorious steeping ginger wafts through the house, energizing me with its aroma. Our shared addiction for our morning chai has become quite comical: even if we have a flight to catch at 3am, we will schedule our alarm clocks earlier to allocate enough time to enjoy our chai before leaving the house. And when we travel, we take the ingredients along with us so that we never miss a day!

The special ingredient (in north Indian chai) has to be the freshly grated ginger, which in itself has many health benefits. The spicy root in the hot, milk-based tea goes back centuries. I use loose tea from India, but you can purchase great-quality tea leaves (mamri chai) from your local Indian store.

I strongly encourage you to reconsider nipping down to your local coffee shop for a morning latte and instead try brewing your own masala chai at home. It will benefit your wallet and your overall health, too.

Serves 4
Prep time: 5 minutes
Cook time: 15 minutes

1 litre/32fl oz/4 cups water

4 tbsp freshly grated ginger

3 tbsp plus 2 tsp loose tea (mamri chai) or 5 black tea bags

4 tsp sugar

320ml/10¾fl oz/1⅓ cups full-fat (whole) milk

Bring the water to the boil in a saucepan. Add the ginger, tea and sugar and cook for 8–10 minutes over a medium-high heat. Add the milk and bring back to the boil. Reduce the heat and simmer over a medium heat for 2 minutes, then bring back to the boil. Repeat this boiling and simmering process twice more until you notice a pink shade to the mixture.

Strain the chai and serve hot. (This is the perfect opportunity to use the fine china!)

Note: If you prefer a thinner chai, use only 240ml/8fl oz/1 cup milk.

SKINNY MANGO LASSI

GF Q

Creamy, heavenly mango lassi – but without the guilty calories! Traditional mango lassi has tons of yogurt, sugar and even ice cream at times! By combining milk and mango pulp, this leaner version is a delight, with its creamy texture and sharp fruity tang from the sweet mango. The crunchy nuts add textural interest.

Serves 2–4
Prep time: 5 minutes

Canned mango pulp, available in Indian stores, should be chilled for several hours in the fridge before use.

950ml/32fl oz/4 cups full-fat (whole) milk

450g/1lb/2 cups canned mango pulp, chilled

30g/1oz/¼ cup cashew nuts, roughly chopped (optional)

Combine the milk and the mango pulp in a blender and blend well until the mixture is fully incorporated. Pour the mixture into glasses and garnish with the chopped cashew nuts, if using.

COCONUT DELIGHT
PAAN MUKHWAS LADOOS

GF Q

I'm so grateful that a friend introduced me to this unusual dish. It took some confidence and a slight modification on my part to confidently serve it to guests.

I love this dish because it's a fantastic palate cleanser (it can be served between courses or after the meal). Whichever way you choose to enjoy it – it's a popular dish; I often take it along to a potluck dinner.

The recipe features gulkand, a sweet and fragrant rose petal jam, which can be found in Indian or Middle Eastern supermarkets.

Makes 12
Prep time: 15 minutes
Cook time: 10 minutes

For the ladoos
4–5 betel leaves (paan), 1cm (½ inch) trimmed on both sides of the stem and roughly chopped

125ml/4fl oz/½ cup condensed (sweetened condensed) milk

1 tbsp ghee or unsalted butter

115g/4oz/1 cup coconut powder

2 tbsp milk

For the filling
1 tbsp dried edible rose petals, crumbled

5 tsp gulkand (rose petal jam)

1 tbsp fennel seeds

1 tsp green cardamom seeds (see Note)

To finish
1 tsp ghee or unsalted butter

55g/2oz/½ cup coconut powder, for coating

Place the betel leaves in a blender or a food processor along with the condensed milk. Blitz for 1–2 minutes and set aside.

Heat the ghee or unsalted butter in a pan over a medium-low heat. Add the coconut powder and cook for 2–3 minutes. Tip in the condensed milk mixture and the milk and stir well to combine. Cook for 4–6 minutes and allow the mixture to thicken. Remove the pan from the heat and set aside to cool a little.

In the meantime, make the filling by simply combining all the ingredients in a bowl.

To finish, grease your hands with ghee and take a small portion of the ladoo mixture. Flatten it and add 1 teaspoon of filling in the centre. Bring the edges together and roll into a ball. Repeat the process until all the ladoos are made.

Roll them in a bowl of coconut powder and store in the fridge as a lovely after-dinner treat!

Note: Cardamom seeds can be extracted from the pods. Using a pestle and mortar, crush the pods lightly and pick out the seeds.

BAKED YOGURT WITH MANGO
MISHTI DOI

GF Q

I was inspired by this dessert when visiting the Maldives one year. The locals and staff were warm, wonderful and welcoming people, and the trip, overall, was in a word, mind-blowing.

When you're strapped for time and want to make a lasting impression, this Bengali dessert is a perfect option to make ahead. All you need is 15 minutes preparation time and it can be chilling in the fridge until you're ready to serve. I always believe you can 'taste the love' when something is homemade, so give this a try before you are tempted to buy a ready-made dessert.

Serves 4
Prep time: 5 minutes +
2 hours chilling
Cook time: 12 minutes

125ml/4fl oz/½ cup condensed (sweetened condensed) milk

125ml/4fl oz/½ cup double (heavy) cream

110g/3¾oz/½ cup plain full-fat yogurt

2 tbsp mango pulp

Preheat the oven to 160°C fan/180°C/350°F/gas mark 4.

Mix all the ingredients in a medium-sized bowl until well combined. Pour the mixture into an ovenproof ceramic bowl and place in the oven for 12 minutes. Remove the bowl from the oven and allow to cool before placing in the fridge for at least 2 hours. Serve chilled.

QUICK ELAICHI SHRIKHAND

GF

Serves 4
Prep time: 10 minutes +
1–2 hours chilling

As a native Gujarati, it's understandable that I am a fan of elaichi shrikhand (strained yogurt). You can use store-bought strained yogurt, or see page 37 for how you can make your own. This dish is traditionally a special-occasion dessert, served at formal events. It's an uncomplicated dessert that delivers on flavour and texture. A quick combination of ingredients with one hour of fridge time – one would never imagine this is a dessert normally reserved for VIPs…

215g/7½oz/1 cup Strained Yogurt
  (page 37)

60g/2 oz/½ cup Cool Whip
  (see Note)

2 tbsp icing (powdered) sugar

½ tsp ground cardamom

2–3 tbsp charoli or sliced pistachio
  nuts or toasted almonds

2–3 tsp slightly crushed dried
  edible rose petals (optional)

½ tsp cardamom seeds,
  crushed (optional)

Pooris (page 167) or chapatis,
  to serve

Place the strained yogurt in a bowl and add the Cool Whip and icing sugar. Whisk well for 2–3 minutes until smooth. Add the ground cardamom and whisk until evenly incorporated.

Pour the mixture into a bowl and garnish with the charoli, and rose petals and cardamom, if using. Place in the fridge for 1 hour before serving with pooris or chapatis.

Note: If you can't get Cool Whip, simply whip up some double (heavy) cream in a metal bowl and, once it is starting to thicken, whisk in some sugar and a couple of drops of vanilla extract. Refrigerate for 2 hours to chill.

CLASSIC GUJARATI: SHRIKHAND

Milk has always been the basic ingredient of many traditional Indian sweets. But milk goes bad if left in warm weather for too long. So to make sweets Indian cooks would simmer milk for a long time, stirring it continuously until it solidified into small balls, called khoya. This is the base of all traditional Indian sweets, such as pedas and barfi. Alternatively, milk would be fermented into curd and then the curd strained so all the moisture drains off.

A large part of Gujarat is desert. Back in the day, nomads needed a way to preserve milk from going sour. They would make a lightweight yogurt and strain it overnight in a cheesecloth pouch. This soft strained yogurt is the basis of shrikhand, one of Gujarat's most beloved desserts. It's especially tasty with hot roti (page 168) or pooris (page 167).

SWEET DUMPLINGS IN ROSE SUGAR SYRUP

GULAB JAMUNS

This traditional Indian dessert is often made during festivals and usually with khoya (milk solids). However, I have opted to use skimmed milk powder instead, with excellent results. A friend first shared this recipe with me, and my mother-in-law insists they are even better than those found in India! My family is equally fond of this sweet treat, and it's become a tradition that I make it for the popular annual Rakhi festival known as Raksha Bandhan, which celebrates brother- or sisterhood.

Serves 4
Prep time: 20 minutes +
4–6 hours soaking
Cook time: 15 minutes

For the flavoured syrup

300g/10½oz/1½ cups sugar

240ml/8fl oz/1 cup water

½ tsp ground cardamom

2 drops rose essence or
  1 tbsp rosewater

For the jamuns

65g/2¼oz/½ cup plain
  (all-purpose) flour

80g/2¾oz/1 cup skimmed
  (fat-free) milk powder

½ tsp baking powder

3 tsp oil, plus 700–950ml/24–
  32fl oz/3–4 cups for deep-frying

60ml/2fl oz/¼ cup double (heavy)
  cream, plus extra if desired for a
  softer texture

dried edible rose petals, to garnish
  (optional)

vanilla ice cream or Rabri (page
  198), to serve (optional)

Make the syrup by placing the sugar and water in a saucepan. Cook over a medium heat for 7–8 minutes or until the mixture becomes a sticky syrup. Whisk in the ground cardamom and rose essence. Remove the pan from the heat and allow it to cool. Transfer the cooled syrup into a suitable lidded container and set aside.

For the jamuns, sift the flour, milk powder and baking powder into a bowl. Mix well, add the oil and cream and combine until the mixture comes together. Knead until the dough is soft and smooth. Grease your hands with a little oil and form 8 round balls from the dough. Shape into smooth walnut-sized shapes with no visible cracks, and place on a tray. Cover with a clean, damp cloth or place in an airtight container. It's important that they do not dry out.

Heat the oil in a wok over a medium heat. When the oil is ready (test with a small piece of dough first), drop 4 of the dumplings into the oil. They will float to the top and double in size. Turn them frequently using a slotted spoon or skimmer until they are golden brown on all sides, about 1½–2 minutes. (Do not allow the oil to become too hot, or they will burn on the outside and remain raw in the centre.) Remove the cooked dumplings with the slotted spoon and drain on a tray lined with paper towels. Repeat the process with the remaining dumplings.

Allow the jamuns to cool, then place in the container of flavoured syrup. Cover with a lid and allow the dumplings to soak for 4–6 hours, where they will soften. Serve with vanilla ice cream or rabri, either as they are or gently reheated in the microwave.

Drinks & Desserts

DESSERT PANCAKES

MALPUA WITH RABRI AND SUKHA MEVA

Serves 4–5
Prep time: 20 minutes +
2 hours chilling + 4–6 hours
cooling and soaking
Cook time: 1 hour 45 minutes

In 2012 I took a special trip to north India with my elder daughter. It ended with a memorable visit to a friend in Delhi, who made malpua with rabri, and it was quite simply one of the best Indian dishes I had ever tasted. I had to rely on memory to recreate it and, after much trial and error, this is the result.

For the flavoured nuts
12 shelled pistachios, roughly
  chopped or thinly sliced

1 tsp ground cardamom

½ tsp saffron powder

For the rabri
1.4 litres/48fl oz/6 cups full-fat
  (whole) milk

3–4 green cardamom pods, crushed

4–5 saffron threads or pinch of
  saffron powder

3½ tbsp sugar

For the malpuas
35g/1¼oz/¼ cup plain
  (all-purpose) flour

80g/2¾oz/1 cup skimmed
  (fat-free) milk powder

2 tbsp coarse semolina (sooji)

½ tsp baking powder

3 tsp oil, plus extra for frying

3–4 tbsp double (heavy) cream

1 quantity Flavoured Syrup
  (page 196)

For the flavoured nuts, simply place the pistachios in a bowl along with the ground cardamom and saffron. Combine well until the nuts are evenly coated in the spices. Set aside.

For the rabri, bring the milk to the boil in a heavy-bottomed saucepan. Add the crushed cardamom pods and saffron and reduce the heat. Cover and simmer for 1 hour 30 minutes until the milk has reduced and thickened. Stir regularly to avoid the milk burning. Remove the pan from the heat and allow it to cool. Whisk in the sugar to dissolve and transfer the mixture to a bowl. Cover and place in the fridge for 2 hours. (Add a little more sugar if you prefer a sweeter end result.)

To make the malpuas, sift the flour, milk powder, semolina and baking powder into a bowl. Use your hands to mix well, then add the oil and cream and combine until the mixture comes together. Knead until the dough is soft and smooth. Grease your hands with a little oil and form 8–10 round balls from the dough. Using a rolling pin, roll the balls into flat circular shapes, approximately 5cm (2 inches) in diameter.

To finish, pan-fry the malpuas in batches. Heat a non-stick frying pan or skillet over a low heat. Once hot, add 2 tablespoons oil and place 2–3 malpuas in the pan. Scatter over ½ teaspoon of the flavoured nuts and press gently so they stick to the malpuas. Cook for 1½ minutes on each side until light golden brown on both sides. Remove and place on a tray lined with paper towels. Repeat the process with the remaining malpuas.

Allow the malpuas to cool down for 1–2 hours. Place them in the container of flavoured syrup after they have completely cooled. Cover with a lid and allow the malpuas to soak for 3–4 hours. Reheat them in the microwave for 1 minute before serving with cold rabri.

KHEER WITH CHERRIES

GF

This special recipe was handed down to me by a Punjabi friend whose mother was one of the greatest cooks I have ever known. I had an outdoor summer party one year and she brought this popular dessert along. I laughed as I read all the 'Thank You' notes from my guests afterwards commenting on the kheer, and had to reveal to them that it was in fact brought by a guest. The feedback obviously sparked my desire to learn how to make it myself and she taught me in her own kitchen. I love it because it was handed down by a friend's mother – it is all the more special because there is likely a beautiful history behind it for her.

Serves 4
Prep time: 10 minutes + 1 hour soaking + 2 hours chilling
Cook time: 1 hour

Be sure to arrange the cherries attractively on top (cut-side up works) and enjoy the creamy, nutty delicious flavours. While this is ideal for summer parties, it's actually suitable all year round because I use Maraschino cherries.

1.4 litres/48fl oz/6 cups full-fat (whole) milk

120g/4¼oz/1 cup cooked basmati rice

3–5 saffron threads

5 green cardamom pods, lightly crushed

10 raisins (optional)

5 tbsp sugar

To decorate
15–20 raw almonds

6 Maraschino cherries, pitted and halved

First, soak the raw almonds, which you will use to decorate. Bring 240ml/8fl oz/1 cup water to the boil in a small pan. Turn off the heat, drop in the almonds and leave to soak for 1 hour. Drain, then peel and slice the almonds and set aside.

Heat the milk in a saucepan over a medium heat. Once the milk starts boiling, reduce the heat to low and add the cooked rice, saffron and crushed cardamom. Stir well and cover the pan tightly with a lid. Cook for 1 hour over a low heat (lifting the lid to give it a quick stir every 10–15 minutes before placing the lid back on again). Never allow cream to rise to the surface – if it does, mix well with the mixture again.

Add the raisins, if using, remove the pan from the heat and allow it to cool. Stir in the sugar and mix well. Put into a bowl, cover and place in the fridge for 2 hours.

Serve chilled, decorated with the sliced almonds. Arrange the halved cherries attractively on the surface.

SAPOTA PUDDING

CHICKOO HALWA

GF Q

Serves 4
Prep time: 10 minutes
Cook time: 20 minutes

250g/9oz/1½ cups chickoo
(sapodilla/sapota), thawed
if frozen

7 tbsp icing (powdered) sugar

1 tbsp ghee

225g/8oz/1 cup grated mawa
(khoya/milk solids), see Note

2–3 drops rose essence (or
1 tbsp rosewater or 2–3 drops
chickoo essence)

3 tbsp roughly chopped cashew
nuts, to decorate

I was first introduced to this dish as a small child. I fell in love 'at first bite' and wanted to learn how to make it myself once it started trending in confectioners (halwais) in Gujarat. According to Gujarati custom, a meal is simply not complete unless there is a sweet element on the plate. As a dessert, it's light and therefore a suitable option after a heavy meal. Chickoo is a fruit rich in vitamin A and calcium with the added benefit of being a good source of fibre. It has a unique flavour and it's worth a trip to your local Indian store to source it. If you cannot find fresh chickoo, it can often be found frozen.

Peel the chickoos and remove the seeds. Place in a blender and blitz until smooth.

Heat a non-stick frying pan or skillet and cook the chickoo purée for 5 minutes over a low heat, stirring continuously. Add the icing sugar and cook for 10 minutes until the mixture has reduced and thickened completely, while stirring occasionally to avoid the mixture sticking to the bottom of the pan. Stir in the ghee and cook for another 2 minutes.

Add the mawa and the rose essence or rosewater, combine thoroughly and cook for 2 minutes while stirring continuously. Pour the mixture into a dish and allow to cool before serving, either at room temperature or in the fridge. Serve decorated with the chopped cashew nuts.

Note: If you can't find mawa, it's really easy to make your own. Simply bring 1.2 litres/40fl oz/5 cups full-fat (whole) milk to the boil in a heavy-bottomed non-stick saucepan. Reduce the heat to low, cover the pan, and simmer for 1 hour, until the milk has reduced and thickened. Keep stirring as you cook, scraping the bottom and sides of the pan to prevent the milk from burning, until the liquid becomes solid. It should have a thick, grainy texture. If necessary, cook for 10–15 minutes more, to achieve the right consistency. Remove the pan from the heat and allow the milk solids to cool. The mixture will solidify further as it cools.

RUBY RED ROSE SORBET

GF DF VG

Serves 4
Prep time: 10 minutes +
10–12 hours freezing
Cook time: 5 minutes

6 tbsp sugar

60ml/2fl oz/¼ cup water

1 tsp fresh lime juice

2 drops rose essence or 1 tbsp
rosewater

240ml/8fl oz/1 cup fresh
pomegranate juice, or use
store-bought

75g/2¾oz/½ cup fresh
pomegranate seeds

To decorate
35g/1¼oz/¼ cup chopped
pistachios

2 tbsp dried edible rose
petals (optional)

I tried a heavenly sorbet much like this one in Paris. Our taxi
driver took us to a patisserie and insisted I tried the rose sorbet.
Stubbornly I refused at first, but then fell in love with this treat
once I tried it. Our waiter generously shared the main ingredients
with me, but I had to figure the rest out on my return home.
The combination of rose and pomegranate is outstanding, and so
is the vibrant colour. I garnish my sorbet with fresh rose petals
from my garden. They are edible because they are chemical-free.
I advise you use store-bought edible rose petals, unless you are
certain your home-grown rose bushes are chemical-free and
organic. Simply pick the petals, wash thoroughly and leave to dry.
It's a fat-free, light, refreshing and very pretty dessert – ideal for
romantic occasions like Valentine's Day.

Place the sugar and water in a pan and bring to the boil. Reduce the
heat to medium-low and cook for 5 minutes, whisking regularly, until
the sugar has fully dissolved. Remove the pan from the heat, add the
lime juice and allow to cool completely.

Once cooled, add the rose essence or rosewater, pomegranate juice and
seeds. Mix well and pour into a freezerproof container. Cover and place
in the freezer for 6 hours until frozen. Take out of the freezer and use a
fork to break the mixture up. Then freeze again for another 4–6 hours,
or until fully frozen.

Scoop the sorbet into serving bowls and garnish with the chopped
pistachios and edible rose petals, if using.

CHURMA LADOO

Churma ladoo holds such wonderful memories for me growing up. My dad was assigned the task of sourcing the best jaggery (gur) he could find, testing it for sweetness, and my grandfather would supply us with ladoo made from pure desi ghee. My mother and grandmother would get to work making the dish together, mostly for special occasions.

The spices and nutty sweetness from the dates complement each other beautifully.

Serves 4
Prep time: 15 minutes
Cook time: 15 minutes

100g/3½oz/¾ cup wholemeal (wholewheat) flour

85g/3oz/½ cup coarse semolina (sooji)

6 tbsp melted ghee, plus 350ml/ 12fl oz/1½ cups for deep-frying (or use oil)

4 tbsp warm water

¼ tsp ground nutmeg

½ tsp ground cardamom

8–10 dried, pitted dates (kharekh), cut into 1cm (½-inch) pieces lengthways

60g/2oz/⅓ cup grated jaggery (gur) or brown sugar

3 tbsp white poppy seeds (optional)

Combine the wholemeal flour, semolina and 4 tablespoons of the melted ghee in a medium bowl and mix well. Add the warm water and knead the dough until the flour is fully incorporated and the dough is soft. Add another 1–2 tablespoons water if needed. Divide the dough into 8 equal-sized portions and shape into a smooth ovals, approximately 7.5cm (3 inches) long.

Heat the ghee for deep-frying in a deep pan over a medium heat. Place 4 portions at a time (unless you have a pan big enough for all 8) into the hot ghee and fry for 5 minutes until golden brown on all sides. Remove with a slotted spoon or skimmer and drain on a tray lined with paper towels. Repeat the process with the remaining 4 portions.

Allow them to cool completely, then place in a food processor and blitz for 5 minutes to a coarse consistency (churma). Transfer to a bowl, add the ground nutmeg and cardamom and mix well. Set aside.

Heat the remaining 2 tablespoons of ghee in a clean pan over a low heat. Add the dates and fry for a minute. Remove the dates from the ghee and set aside. Now add the jaggery and mix well with the ghee, cooking for 20–30 seconds over a very low heat. Once you notice the jaggery bubbling in the ghee, remove the pan from the heat. Pour the melted jaggery into the reserved churma mixture and combine well.

Divide the mixture into 8–10 equal portions, shaping each one into a ball. While shaping, slide a piece of date into the centre of each ladoo, hiding it completely. Put the poppy seeds on a plate, if using, then roll the ladoo in it. Serve.

Drinks & Desserts

INDEX

A

adzuki bean patties 68
Ahmedabad 14
ajwain/ajmo (carom) seeds 21
Amritsari chole 143
appetizers (farsans) 15, 63–107
asafoetida 21
aubergines (eggplants):
  pan-fried aubergine curry 131
  smoky aubergine 137
  surti undhiyu 162–3

B

bajra flour 21
baked spicy cakes 96–7
beans 123
beansprouts: papadum salad 58
beetroot: sunset beetroot
    salad 59
  tapioca red pearls delight 183
besan (gram or chickpea) flour 21
  besan and fenugreek fritters 72
  besan chutney 40
  chickpea rolls 66
  green pepper and besan
    masala 130
  layered taro leaves 100
  spinach dumplings 91
  yellow sponges 77
betel leaves: coconut delight 191
bhakhri 166, 175
black gram/black chickpeas 21
  chickpea patties 85
black onion seeds/nigella seeds 21
breads 165–77
  bhakhri 166, 175
  dhebra 172
  double-layered roti 170
  papadum curry 150
  papadum salad 58
  pav bhaji 157–9
  pearl millet bread 176
  poori 167, 175
  roti 168, 175
  rotlo 175
  sweet lentil bread 169
  tapioca paratha 174
burnt garlic rice 181
butter (lima) beans:

butter beans in jaggery and
    tamarind 153
  Indian beans in green curry 140
  surti undhiyu 162–3

C

cardamom 21–3
cashew nuts: cashew curry 146
  cashew paste 35
  flattened rice with nut and
    spice 99
cauliflower: cauliflower and potato
    nu shaak 128
  cauliflower with curry leaves 139
chaat, spinach 61
chaat powder 23
chai, masala 188
charoli nuts 23
cheese:
  green goddess chutney pizza 83
  see also paneer
cherries, kheer with 199
chickoo (sapodilla/sapota):
  sapota pudding 200
chickpea flour see besan
chickpea patties 85
chickpea rolls 66
chickpeas, dried (garbanzo beans):
  Amritsari chole 143
  chickpea crumble cake 86
  dakor na gota 75
  samosa soup 120
chickpeas, fresh (garbanzo beans):
  green chickpea salad 52
chillies 23
  green chilli paste 32
  khaman chutney 77
churma ladoo 202
chutney: besan chutney 40
  chutney pulao 185
  curry leaf chutney 44
  green garlic chutney 41
  khaman chutney 77
  mint chutney 42
  peanut chutney 43
  sweet tamarind chutney 45
cilantro see coriander
cluster beans with sesame
    seeds 149

coconut 23
  coconut delight 191
coriander (cilantro):
  green paste 30
  khaman chutney 77
coriander seeds 23
  coriander-cumin powder 29
corn delight 81
corn fritters 70
courgettes (zucchini): baked spicy
    cakes 96–7
cracked wheat khichdi 180
croquettes: spicy pea croquettes 88
  spicy potato croquettes 98
cumin seeds 23
  coriander-cumin powder 29
curries 127–63
  Amritsari chole 143
  cashew curry 146
  cauliflower and potato
    nu shaak 128
  cauliflower with curry leaves 139
  cluster beans with sesame
    seeds 149
  curried runner beans 144–5
  easy-peasy potato curry 142
  garlic and potato curry 132
  green pepper and besan
    masala 130
  guava in gravy 152
  Indian beans in green curry 140
  pan-fried aubergine curry 131
  papadum curry 150
  pav bhaji 157–9
  potato and pea curry 134
  simple butter paneer 155
  smoky aubergine 137
  surti undhiyu 162–3
  taro and ridge gourd curry 160
curry leaves 23
  curry leaf chutney 44

D

dakor na gota 75
dal 123
  creamy masoor dal 112
  easy dal 117
  Gujarati dal 118
  red lentil dal 114

dates 23–4
  churma ladoo 202
dessert pancakes 198
dhana-jeeru 29
dhebra 172
dhokla, white 80
double-layered roti 170
drinks:
  masala chai 188
  skinny mango lassi 190
dumplings:
  fenugreek dumplings 144–5
  spinach dumplings 91
  sweet dumplings in rose sugar
    syrup 196

E
easy dal 117
easy-peasy potato curry 142
edamame beans: chutney
    pulao 185
eggplants see aubergines
eggs, spiced scrambled 138
elaichi shrikhand 194
Eno (fruit salt) 24

F
farsans (appetizers) 15, 63–107
fennel seeds 24
fenugreek leaves 24
  besan and fenugreek fritters 72
  dhebra 172
  fenugreek dumplings 144–5
fenugreek seeds 24
fenugreek sprouts 35
  papadum curry with 150
flattened rice with nut and spice 99
fritters:
  besan and fenugreek fritters 72
  corn fritters 70
  crispy samosas 102
  crispy taro potli 101
  okra fries 84
  spicy pea croquettes 88

G
garbanzo beans see chickpeas
garlic: burnt garlic rice 181
  garlic and potato curry 132
  garlic paste 31
  green garlic chutney 41

green goddess chutney pizza 83
  red garlic chutney 94–5
  spicy garlic soup 122
garlic scapes 24
ghee 24–5
ginger paste 32
gram flour see besan
grapes: green grape and tomato
    salad 55
green goddess chutney pizza 83
green paste 30
guava in gravy 152
Gujarati dal 118

I
Indian beans in green curry 140
ingredients 21–7

J
jaggery 25

K
kachumber, mango and
    red onion 49
Kathiyawad 14
khaman chutney 77
kheer with cherries 199
khichdi 180, 184
Kutch 14
Kutchi dabeli 94–5

L
lassi, skinny mango 190
legumes 123
lentil bread 169
lentils (masoor dal) 27
  creamy masoor dal 112
  red lentil dal 114
lima beans see butter beans

M
mangoes:
  baked yogurt with mango 193
  mango and red onion
    kachumber 49
  quick and easy mango pickle 46
  skinny mango lassi 190
masala chai 188
milk 194
  dessert pancakes 198
  kheer with cherries 199

masala chai 188
  skinny mango lassi 190
millet: pearl millet bread 176
mint chutney 42
mung beans, split (mung/
    moong dal) 25
  cracked wheat khichdi 180
mustard seeds 25

O
okra fries 84
onions: mango and red onion
    kachumber 49
  samosa soup 120
  smoky aubergine 137

P
pancakes: dessert pancakes 198
  yellow pancakes 104
paneer: paneer tikka 92
  simple butter paneer 155
papadum curry 150
papadum salad 58
paratha, tapioca 174
patties: adzuki bean patties 68
  baked spicy cakes 96–7
  chickpea patties 85
  Kutchi dabeli 94–5
pav bhaji 157–9
peanuts: peanut chutney 43
  spiced peanuts 94–5
pearl millet bread 176
peas: pav bhaji 157–9
  potato and pea curry 134
  spicy pea croquettes 88
peppers (bell): green pepper and
    besan masala 130
  pav bhaji 157–9
pickles: pickle masala 34
  quick and easy mango pickle 46
pigeon peas, dried split (toor
    dal) 24
  baked spicy cakes 96–7
  easy dal 117
  Gujarati dal 118
  spicy garlic soup 122
  sweet lentil bread 169
  yellow rice 184
pigeon peas, fresh (tuver lilva) 27
  surti undhiyu 162–3
pizza, green goddess chutney 83

pomegranate juice: ruby red rose
    sorbet 201
poori 167, 175
poppy seeds 26
potatoes: cauliflower and potato
    nu shaak 128
  crispy samosas 102
  deep-fried potatoes 69
  easy-peasy potato curry 142
  garlic and potato curry 132
  Kutchi dabeli 94–5
  potato and pea curry 134
  spicy potato croquettes 98
  surti undhiyu 162–3
  tapioca paratha 174
pulao, chutney 185

R
raita, yogurt 56
rasam: spicy garlic soup 122
red lentil dal 114
rice 179–85
  baked spicy cakes 96–7
  burnt garlic rice 181
  chutney pulao 185
  flattened rice with
    nut and spice 99
  kheer with cherries 199
  yellow rice 184
rice flour 26
  steamed rice flour 78
  yellow pancakes 104
ridge gourds: taro and ridge
    gourd curry 160
rose essence 26–7
  ruby red rose sorbet 201
  sweet dumplings in rose sugar
    syrup 196
roti 168, 175
  double-layered roti 170
rotlo 175
ruby red rose sorbet 201
runner beans:
  curried runner beans 144–5
  surti undhiyu 162–3

S
sago: tapioca paratha 174
  tapioca red pearls delight 183
salads: green chickpea salad 52
  green grape and tomato salad 55

papadum salad 58
  sunset beetroot salad 59
salt 14
samosa soup 120
samosas, crispy 102
sapota pudding 200
semolina: white dhokla 80
sesame seeds, cluster beans
    with 149
shrikhand, quick elaichi 194
skinny mango lassi 190
sorbet, ruby red rose 201
soups: samosa soup 120
  spiced yogurt soup 125
  spicy garlic soup 122
spinach: spinach chaat 61
  spinach dumplings 91
spring roll wrappers: crispy taro
    potli 101
sugar 14–15
Surat 14
surti lilva 27
  Indian beans in green curry 140
  surti undhiyu 162–3
surti papdi 27
  surti undhiyu 162–3
sweet lentil bread 169
sweet potatoes: surti undhiyu
    162–3
sweetcorn: corn delight 81
  corn fritters 70

T
tamarind: butter beans in jaggery
    and tamarind 153
  sweet tamarind chutney 45
  tamarind purée 36
tapioca paratha 174
tapioca red pearls delight 183
taro leaves: crispy taro potli 101
  layered taro leaves 100
  taro and ridge gourd curry 160
tea 27
  masala chai 188
temperatures, cooking 20
thali 106
tikka, paneer 92
tofu: burnt garlic rice 181
tomatoes: Amritsari chole 143
  cashew curry 146
  green grape and tomato salad 55

Gujarati dal 118
  pan-fried aubergine curry 131
  pav bhaji 157–9
  simple butter paneer 155
  smoky aubergine 137
  tomato purée 36
turmeric 27

V
valor papdi 27
vegetarianism 13

W
wheat (bulgur): cracked wheat
    khichdi 180
white dhokla 80

Y
yam: surti undhiyu 162–3
yellow pancakes 104
yellow rice 184
yellow sponges 77
yogurt:
  baked yogurt with mango 193
  quick elaichi shrikhand 194
  spiced yogurt soup 125
  spinach chaat 61
  strained yogurt 37
  white dhokla 80
  yogurt raita 56

Z
zucchini see courgettes

ACKNOWLEDGEMENTS

This book is not only a collection of recipes, but a collection of unforgettable moments we have spent together as a family, so I simply must start by thanking them. Cooking for my kids and husband is the most fun thing for me, and I wish I could do this for the rest of my life. Love always!

Our elder daughter, Elissa: the initial driving force behind the book. It began as a suggestion in 2017. She came around for supper one night and put the idea in my head – and in my heart. A picky eater all her life, this was the greatest compliment I could have received. Like a dog with a bone, she never relented and continued to set deadlines for me, giving me no other choice than to create this book. I recall the first recipe I finished for this book was sweet dal (and I even remember the date: 19 September 2017.) Elissa instilled confidence in me and gave me a new purpose, a new direction, a fire in my belly. Thank you, beautiful girl – your positivity and happy outlook on life are infectious. You still win the award for Drama Queen!

Our son, Aamir: never failing to encourage me daily, reinforcing the idea that this was going to be a masterpiece. He is forever my well-wisher, offering patient guidance and support. His lovingly delivered lectures did not go unheard or unappreciated. I love you my sunny boy!

Our youngest, Ravina: lecturing me regularly on the importance of social media and offering honest and open advice. She would often send me hilarious texts of encouragement, allowing her creative side to shine as she enquired about the progress of the book. While still focusing on her schoolwork, she never failed to remember this family project. Ravina, I am so proud of the woman you are becoming – stay as sweet as you are!

For my darling husband, Haresh, who played the greatest supporting role. It is difficult to find the right words to thank you appropriately. Much like a Gujarati meal is followed by something sweet, so are your words of support, love and praise. Your positive attitude and endless good energy kept me motivated and made this journey all the more meaningful and exciting. I know you say that you do not have a sensitive nose, but somehow you always manage to smell my food! I love it when you let me know what meals you are most looking forward to on returning home after a trip away, or indeed claiming to be the first one allowed at any leftovers! You always made me feel my cooking was better than any restaurant and I will always be grateful for you instilling that confidence in me. You know my heart so well and are a true friend. I know I speak for our beautiful children (and the extended families) when I say that you are a blessing to us, and we are all so proud of you. You are the true hero of this book. We will continue to spice up our relationship. You absolute rock, I love you.

To my dearest friend and culinary editor across the pond, Monya Kilian Palmer: I quickly developed a great relationship with her. She understood my passion from the very beginning and brought my words to life. She understood my vision and would capture my 'voice' throughout the book.

In April 2019 I took a chance and sent my all-time favourite food photographer Jonathan Lovekin an email. Imagine my delight when this world-class photographer responded and agreed to work on my project! I was dancing like a kid in a candy store, beaming from ear to ear as I shared the news with my family! Not only did he fly in from London to capture the dishes over the course of a week, but he secured a food stylist and advised on the ideal props to use. Jonathan, you are a patient and respectful man, a wonderful soul, a multi-tasking super-human! Thank you for going above and beyond for me. It was an incredibly memorable experience for me and right up there as one of the best weeks of my life. I will never forget the things you taught me. Indeed, it was an additional honour to feed you that week and share my recipes with you following our time together.

To Aubri, who shared so much knowledge about using props. Many thanks. To Claire and Dave, thank you for allowing us the opportunity to shoot in your space. Your facility is top-notch, and I fell in love with all your props! Gabriella, my trusted housekeeper for many years – thank you for never hesitating when I needed assistance. I could count on you during the photoshoot process, where you ensured the kitchen was always spotless for the food shots. Thank you to Sourish: you took incredibly special care of us. We will always treasure those delicious Gujarati breakfasts (always plenty of sugar!). Thank you for the positive and blessed experience, and for all the spoils and brilliant hospitality – you represent the spirit of Gujarat! My darling niece, Sona, your support and assistance were so helpful when getting permission from vendors for photoshoots.

Thank you Sandhya for your valuable time and input.

To dear friends Jason, Priya V., Purnima, Preeti G., Kiran M., Dolly, Mayuranki, Krishna D.– I was humbled and impressed at the amount of support you offered me and all the kind and wonderful people who helped in some way or another throughout this journey, I promise I will do my very best to bring the wonderful Gujarati food and culture for all the world to see. I poured my heart and soul into this book, but it would not have been possible without all the love and creativity from everyone involved. Lastly, so many family and friends around the world shared their authentic recipes with me; I will always appreciate your generosity of time and patience. And, to the many lovely, humble people of Gujarat who willingly shared their recipes and tips with me without hesitation, I couldn't be more grateful. Together we can now share Gujarati food with the world, so THIS IS FOR YOU!

Michelle Meade and I met on a bright sunny day in October 2019. It was my lucky day! Michelle's positive energy and belief in my book were a great source of inspiration. She went above and beyond her responsibility, as my agent, to make my cookbook a reality. She was so committed and dedicated to this project and worked tirelessly to find Pavilion. I will be forever grateful to Michelle for all her support and dedication to making this book a success. She has become and will remain a dear friend for life.

My special thanks to Pavilion Books, and especially to Lucy, Helen and the entire team for believing in my cookbook and helping to bring it to life. What a wonderful team to work with. It takes a unique skill set and, more importantly, courage, to believe in and invest in a first-time author. I'm honoured and humbled that such a renowned publisher decided to take on this project and help me bring Gujarati cuisine to kitchens across the world.

Lastly, this is for my father. As my greatest support, you have always inspired me and those in your community. I am so proud to be sharing my heartfelt Gujarati recipes with the world. I miss you.